5/90

3000 800025 18525
St. Louis Community College

D0891520

Portrait of Puerto Rico

Portrait of Puerto Rico

Louise Cripps Samoiloff

Cornwall Books
New York • London • Toronto

Cornwall Books
440 Forsgate Drive
Cranbury, NJ 08512

Cornwall Books
25 Sicilian Avenue
London WC1A 2QH, England

Cornwall Books
2133 Royal Windsor Drive
Unit 1
Mississauga, Ontario, Canada L5J 1K5

Library of Congress Cataloging in Publication Data

Samoiloff, Louise Cripps.
Portrait of Puerto Rico.

Bibliography: p.
Includes index.
1. Puerto Rico. I. Title.
F1958.S2 1982 972.95 77-84585
ISBN 0-8453-4751-9 AACR1

Printed in the United States of America

For Martin Jr., Clayton, Sherman,
Clifton, and Orion,
who have all enjoyed Puerto Rico and for my husband,
who helped me compile this book

Contents

Portrait of Puerto Rico

1
The Taino Ancestors of Puerto Rico

IN 1492, Christopher Columbus first came upon the Caribbean islands. He was impressed with their fair harbors, their trees with beautiful and varied flowers and strange fruits, their extravagant lushness, and extraordinary beauty. He declared there was not a more fertile region in the whole universe. One of his fellow voyagers on first sight of one of those islands, Puerto Rico, called it "a garden for bees," and mentioned its lovely harbors "teeming with fish."

Subsequent voyagers were to praise the beauty of Puerto Rico and term it, with its sister islands, "Paradise."

When Columbus first encountered the natives of the islands, he could not find enough praise for their gentleness, goodness, generosity, and intelligence. When he found that there was gold on the islands, (of Hispaniola, Cuba and Puerto Rico), his enthusiasm knew no bounds. The islands had riches as well as beauty.

Columbus had had difficulty in obtaining support for his first expedition. His belief was that he could, by sailing westward, arrive at the Indies. Here he expected to find many riches, spices, and other desirable products. At that time, the Indies meant China, Japan, Indonesia, and India itself.

For this reason, the area he discovered was called the West Indies and the natives termed West Indians. Until his death, Columbus believed that he had found the East and a westward route to it.

The first island he found was a small one in the Bahamas. After a month at sea, he was grateful to reach land. His supplies were dwindling and his crews were becoming mutinous. He called the island San Salvador, in thanks to the Savior for a safe haven. San Salvador obviously had little to offer in the way of riches. He managed to indicate to the islanders that he was seeking gold, and they told him he would find it not too far away. Taking a couple of natives to act as guides, he again set sail. The natives led him first to Cuba, which he thought was a continent, and then to another large island. This large island, he named Española or Hispaniola, was later divided into Haiti and the Dominican Republic. Here he was warmly welcomed and given many feasts in his honor. He in turn invited one of the chief "caciques," or leaders, on board. He wrote later that the chief acted "with royal poise." During this visit one of his ships went aground. The natives worked diligently to help Columbus salvage as much as possible. Attesting to their scrupulous honesty, he said that not one single "lace-point," or needle, had been stolen. What most delighted him, however, were the gifts of golden objects the natives gave him: two golden statues, a belt with a large gold buckle, and other gold pieces. He also observed that they wore golden earrings, designed in the shapes of leaves and flowers. Most of the natives wore golden nose rings, bracelets, and some collars. They showed him nuggets of gold in the rivers and indicated that he was welcome to take what he wished, since they set no particular store by it.

Gathering up a reasonable amount of gold and other treasures, including forty parrots, he decided not to tarry long in this Paradise, but in triumph to hurry back to Spain. He took five inhabitants for navigators and interpreters and left behind a few dozen men to build an outpost and to explore the island further for gold.

When he returned to Spain with his rapturous tale, there was little difficulty in getting together a second expedition. After Columbus had discovered his western route, this first idea had been to set up trade with the "Indies." But realizing how easy it would be to overcome the gentle natives of the islands by armed force, on his second voyage he took with him 1,200 soldiers and a fleet of seventeen ships.

It was on the second voyage, when he arrived further south in the Caribbean, passing or stopping briefly at many of the islands, which he claimed for the Spanish crown by right of discovery, that he first came upon Borinquén, an island just east of Hispaniola, that he named San Juan Bautista. This was on November 17, 1493. He stayed only three or four days since he was anxious to get back to Hispaniola and further to explore Cuba. But one of his companions on this second expedition, Juan Ponce de Leon, on seeing Puerto Rico, decided that

On his second voyage, Christopher Columbus initially came upon Borinquen (Puerto Rico) on November 17, 1493. (PHOTO COURTESY OF PUERTO RICO TOURISM DEVELOPMENT.)

this was the island he would later make his own territory.

Columbus found on his return to Hispaniola that there was no outpost, and the men he had left behind had died either from disease or had been killed by the natives. His men had grossly abused the hospitality of the natives, raped their women, used their men as

With renewed interest shown in their Taino ancestors, murals with Indian motifs, such as this Indian warrior, are now being painted on a variety of buildings in Puerto Rico. (PHOTO BY JOSÉ GARCIA, SAN JUAN STAR.)

Statue of Juan Ponce de Leon in the plaza named for him in San Juan. He was the first Spanish governor of Puerto Rico. (PHOTO BY FRANK H. WADSWORTH.)

slaves, and demanded more gold and more offerings than the natives were prepared to give. The natives decided they must eliminate the intruders if they were to settle back to their previous peaceful existence.

Columbus now landed with hundreds of men, cannons, guns, harquebuses (shoulder guns), and other weaponry. The bows and arrows and stones flung by the natives were pitiful. Their nakedness contrasted sharply against their armored enemy. They were quickly subdued. Realizing the true nature of these strangers, the natives banded together and fought bravely but unsuccessfully to keep their island free.

The Spaniards were merciless, burning villages, killing men, women, and children. First Hispaniola was conquered and then Cuba. Puerto Rico, during this time had been left unharmed. Now came her turn. The appearance of the Indian warriors as they rushed into battle was fearsome. They made themselves repulsive to frighten their enemies, marching into battle daubed with paint. Their hair, long and black, was twisted into strange forms.

In 1508, Juan Ponce de Leon who had been a foot soldier under Columbus, arrived and later became first governor of Puerto Rico. According to a chronicler of the time (Bartolomé de Las Casas), he was a harsh, cruel man. Fray Bartolomé de Las Casa, who came to the islands with Columbus, writes of Ponce de Leon, "He grew rich on the labor, blood, and sufferings of his subjects." He had taken part in the cruel crushing and victimization of the natives of Hispaniola. The people of Puerto Rico suffered as their fellow tribes on the neighboring islands had suffered. They were torn from a peaceful, life attuned to nature, and forced to work in gold mines and act as slaves to the harsh men who had conquered them.

The natives whom the Spaniards encountered when they discovered the three main islands of the Greater Antilles (Hispaniola, Cuba, and Puerto Rico) were Tainos of the Arawak tribes. "Taino" means gentle. In this, they differed from the Carib tribes to the south in the Lesser Antilles. The Caribs were fierce cannibalistic warriors who made raids on the Arawak people.

How all these tribes came to be living on the islands is now fairly well established. Originally, there is said to have been a migration of people over what is now the Bering Strait, but what was then a land mass. In this and later migrations, the tribes moved down through North, Central, and South America. Those who remained in the northern part of the hemisphere are said to be of a different blood type from those who moved farther down into the south in a second migration. From South America, the tribes moved into the islands.

The great rivers of the Magdellena and Orinoco in the northeast corner of South America in what is now Colombia and Venezuela, produce a current so great that debris is carried for miles towards the Caribbean islands. Men could easily have used the force of the currents either in rafts or log boats to carry them to the first of the islands. They would then move throughout the whole chain of islands that stretches in a westward sweeping arc from Trinidad to Puerto Rico and inward again to Cuba and Jamaica.

The flow of currents in the Straits of Yucatan and Florida swing back northeast to unite in the Gulf Stream. This probably contributed to later migrations to the Greater Antilles, including Puerto Rico.

Early Puerto Rican history repeated in many respects the history of her sister islands of Hispaniola and Cuba. Her roots, her beginnings, like theirs, spread from South America.

The very first migrants from Asia—some say possibly China—probably arrived about 40,000 B.C. Anthropologists studying the Tainos, have found many similarities, especially in art, with Asia and China. And interestingly, Columbus in his diary, describes the Tainos and mentions their "upward slanting eyes." By 5,000 B.C. there were already established corn cultures in South America. On the basis of recent discoveries, anthropologists Cruxent and Rouse of Yale University also believe that by that time there were similar settlements in Puerto Rico and her sister islands.

As Europeans and North Americans look back to the great civilizations of Greece and Rome as the roots of their culture, Puerto Ricans can trace their cultural roots to the great civilization that grew up in Mexico, Central, and South America, to the "mother culture" of the Olmecs, and to the great Aztec and Inca civilizations. The magnificent civilizations that the Spaniards so ruthlessly destroyed in what is now Latin America are part of the Puerto Rican heritage. Perhaps it was only a pale reflection of those civilizations, but it was from there that their culture began. Over the centuries it is from there that those original roots have been continuously nourished. Puerto Ricans today, by their ethnic background, their history, and their language, are still tied to Latin America.

At the time of Columbus's discovery of their island, the people of Puerto Rico, were not just a few savages, who lazed under tropical trees waiting for the fruits to fall into their open mouths. For one thing, "they were skilled agriculturists," according to the early chroniclers. They cultivated their fields with maize, manioc, cassava, some corn, yucca, yams, and other grains and root vegetables. From the former, they made their bread.

Their language, which was sufficiently sophisticated for them to

This stone "petroglyph," was carved by a Taino artist over 600 years ago. The Tainos met Christopher Columbus when he discovered Puerto Rico and they have left important archaeological remains on the island (PHOTO COURTESY OF PUERTO RICO TOURISM DEVELOPMENT.)

discuss such abstract ideas as eternity, was that of the Arawak family, which was spread through Colombia, Amazonia, and Central America. With this means of communication open, there is evidence of continuing contact with the mainland. They acted as interpreters when the Spaniards continued their explorations to the mainland.

Petroglyphs on hard ionite rock in the Rio Blanco Canyon on the south side of the Luquillo Mountains. The petroglyphs show the influence of South American culture. (PHOTO BY FRANK H. WADSWORTH.)

They learned Spanish quickly. Also Arawaks made prisoners by the British learned to speak English so that they might act as interpreters in that language too. So these natives, often described later as "savages," implying small mental capacity, were obviously as Christopher Columbus described them, "men of intelligence."

Besides being agriculturists, the Borinquéns fished, catching different kinds of ocean fish as well as big turtles and various shell fish, whose shells they put to use. They also caught for their meat the huge manatees, who used to feed on the greenery at the mouth of rivers. One town in Puerto Rico on the north shore is still called Manatí after that ancient sea beast.

Another skill of the Borinquéns was the making of pottery. They made pottery to serve their household needs as well as for decorating purposes.

They carved and polished stones and made stone and wooden sculptures to decorate the outside of their houses. Peter Martyr, Counsellor to the King of Spain, writes of "plates, platters, cauldrons, and plates made of black wood, brilliantly polished . . . decorated with representations of phantoms . . . and serpents and men, and every thing they see about them." They drew pictographs on stone slabs and in caves. Their pictographs on the outside of their houses and the houses themselves were again said to show the influence of South America. Carved sniffing tubes of wood have also been discovered which were probably used by their priests for narcotics and tobacco.

They made spoons and trays of wood, knives and hatchets of stone, and pots and bowls of clay. They made stools on which to sit. Many stools were made of carved wood or embellished stone with four short legs and an animal head. In the British Museum in London, there is a beautiful West Indian stool, ornamented, and inlaid with gold. Less elaborate stools were used as grinding mortars.

They slept in hammocks strung across the house. These proved to be comfortable beds which could be rolled up in the morning so that they occupied no space in the daytime. Small hammocks called "coys"

Coco Falls is only one of the natural beauties of El Yunque's rain forest, where the Tainos believed one of their gods resided. Except for the shirt, the little girl sitting on the rock might be an Indian maiden. (PHOTO COURTESY OF PUERTO RICO TOURISM DEVELOPMENT.)

The timeless, harmonious world of Borinquén (Puerto Rico) A typical forest scene in El Yunque, where the Indians believed the "good god" Yuquiqui lived.

were made for the babies. Puerto Ricans in the hills still make "coys" for their babies' cribs.

Use of sails and awnings, decorative designs in paint and carvings—all were traits making the squared off West Indies canoe a highly developed invention. They carried about ninety men, and long paddles were generally used. Long voyages were not infrequent.

When they came aboard Columbus's ships, they brought as gifts, fish, bread, cotton, rabbits, and birds, as well as gifts of gold.

At one end of Borinquén (Puerto Rico) some Spanish sailors "found there a handsome house built in the fashion of the country and surrounded by a dozen or more ordinary structures."

Their houses, according to Columbus, were well-constructed and well-engineered. Tall trees supported by smaller ones were used for the outer wooden posts. "The ceilings were decked with branches of various colors, most artfully plaited together." The "king" of the island was said to have a particularly fine house.

There were plenty of cotton trees on the island and the women spun the cotton and wove it into cloth. Though they wore little or no clothing, some men wore loin cloths, and the older women draped a

The natural world of the Indians. La Mina falls in the rain forest (Caribbean Natural Forest). (PHOTO BY FRANK H. WADSWORTH.)

skirt, sarong fashion, around their hips. They also knew the art of dyeing, so their clothes were of different colors.

"As for the young girls, they covered no part of themselves, but wore their hair loose upon their shoulders and a narrow ribbon tied around their forehead. All were so beautiful one might think they

From time immemorial, the island probably looked like this. Bird Island, off La Parguera, now a rookery for cattle egrets. (PHOTO BY FRANK H. WADSWORTH.)

were those splendid nymphs celebrated by the ancients. Holding branches of palms in their hands, they danced to the accompaniment of songs."

The natives made up songs which they called 'arreytos' told tales, and passed on news and stories through poetry. Columbus tells how he visited a playhouse where a performance was given for him. They had meeting places, usually a square in the center of each village. These were called "bateyes." Today old men in the hills of Puerto Rico will still speak of a "batey" for a place of meeting.

A book of photographs by Marvin W. Schwartz called *Huelles (Traces)* published by the Institute of Puerto Rican Culture show remnants of the culture that existed on the island during the time of the Tainos. The photographs of the natural and creative world of the Indians—of man groves, rivers, forests, waterfalls, mountains, caves, rock carvings and the sculptures of stone, clay and wood—evoke the timeless, harmonious world of Borinquén. Ricardo Alegria, former Director of Cultural Affairs, says in a preface to this book, "Only a few traces remain of the rich and wondrous aboriginal world that was our island." There was at that time a close identification existing between man and nature, between the islander and his island.

Columbus found the Borinquéns to be excellent navigators, using the stars for their compass. This knowledge of navigation caused surprise and admiration among the Spaniards. Columbus and others used the Borinquéns for pilots. Juan Ponce de Leon used them to take him to Florida and to the island of Bimini, where there was supposed to be a Fountain of Youth. According to Aurelio Tió, a Puerto Rican historian, Juan Ponce de Leon had heard not only about medicinal waters in Bimini, but of riches in gold and precious stones. It seems more likely his quest was for the latter, since he was only thirty-six and surely not concerned with old age.

The natives of Puerto Rico and the other islands of the Greater Antilles were aware of the Gulf Stream and its currents, and made use of it to "traverse all the seas around them." By passing on this information to the Spaniards, the latter were helped in reaching Mexico and the resplendent cities of the Aztecs.

The island was fairly thickly populated at the time of the conquest. An early estimate gives the population figure of 600,000. Many dispute this and suggest that there was an error of a zero. Even if this were so, Puerto Rico did not again have a population of as much as 60,000 until 250 years later.

Puerto Rico, like most of the Caribbean islands, is very beautiful. Volcanic eruptions in pre-historic times created mountain ridges and valleys. Puerto Rico is one of the peaks of mostly underwater

Mountains of limestone run like a central backbone through Puerto Rico. (PHOTO BY FRANK H. WADSWORTH.)

Canyon de San Cristobal in the mountainous interior. When Indians were the chief inhabitants the island was densely forested, and had many waterfalls. (PHOTO BY FRANK H. WADSWORTH.)

mountains stretching from Florida to Venezuela. Mountains of limestone run like a central backbone through Puerto Rico.

It is fourth in size among the islands; thirty-six miles wide and 100 miles long, roughly the size of Long Island, New York.

According to the records of the time, these Arawakan Indians were of average height, lightly built, small-boned with long delicate feet and hands and lean muscular bodies. They had slightly slanting, small eyes, straight black hair, and a toast-colored skin. The women were reported to have been very lovely. Amerigo Vespucci wrote glowingly of them: "Venuses of the Caribbean, with their graceful, well-formed bodies, voluptuous and unflagging in their desires." With typical Latin maschismo, he adds, "We greatly took their fancy."

The scientist explorer, Von Humboldt, following Columbus' routes, found the Arawakans of South America, who were still living there in the nineteenth century, to be men of lean muscular bodies, average height, small-boned with straight black hair. Columbus also said they "had long delicate hands and feet."

On the other hand, except for a handful of clergy and noblemen, who captained the ships or came for the adventure and gold, most of the men of the Spanish fleets were brutish. They were illiterate men "who could not even write their names." Also "they were debauchees, profligates, thieves, ravishers. They respected nothing—and were given over to violence and rapine—killing, burning and roasting their victims in cages." An eye-witness, Friar Bartolomé de Las Casas, wrote in *La Historia de Los Indies* of their "laying wagers as to who could most quickly bowel a man in the middle or with one blow of a sword would most readily and most severely cut off his head, or that would best pierce his entrails at one stroke."

Bartolomé de Las Casas wrote works of propaganda "flaming with indignation at the cruelties visited upon the Indians by the Conquistadores," and he went to Spain time and time again to plead their cause at the Royal Court. He had shipped out with Columbus and was given his "encomienda" with the others—that is, his portion of land and some Indians. But the horrors he witnessed led him to take Holy Orders and he became a Dominican friar. His writings were eye-witness accounts collected during his visit to all the islands and later South America and Mexico. He is known as the 'Apostle of the Indians' because of his efforts to stop the enslavement and virtual annihilation of the Indians. He denied the tales of a contemporary

These stones of different sizes and marked by petroglyphs mark the boundaries of the Ceremonial Park where the Tainos played their religious ball games. (PHOTO COURTESY OF INSTITUTO DE CULTURA PUERTORRIQUEÑA.)

Ex-Governor Muñoz Marin walking in the old Indian Ceremonial Park in Utuado with Ricardo Alegria, who was Director of the Instituto Cultura Puertorriqueña. The park is believed to have been constructed in 1,200 A.D. (PHOTO COURTESY OF INSTITUTO DE CULTURA PUERTORRIQUEÑA.)

writer, Oviedo, a fellow colonist, who called Indians sodomists, rapists, and thieves.

Before the Spanish arrived the people of the island had lived in harmony with nature and with each other. They believed in One Supreme Being, but also had lesser gods. They made "cemies," carved stone figures for household talismen, in much the same way that Puerto Ricans in the nineteenth century, as Catholics and believers in One God, made wooden "santos" to be prayed before in their homes. They believed in a heaven and a hell as places where one went after death.

Columbus is said to have been amazed that the naked natives could discuss the question of one's soul and beliefs in an afterlife.

The belt with a golden buckle given to Columbus was probably one used in ceremonial ball games. A ball park in Utuado on the north shore of Puerto Rico, excavated in recent years, is believed to be about 700 years old and constructed in A.D. 1,200. There are fourteen structures consisting of paved walks, plazas, and long parallel lines of heavy stones of varying heights bearing carvings in bas relief. Religious ball games were played both in Mesó-America and Mexico, and existed before 1,000 B.C. The name of the ball, *vike,* means fruit, the fruit of the rubber tree. The ball embodied all the fruits which were brought to a festival. Ball games were played in the villages as well as the special ceremonial grounds. They were probably similar to a form of soccer, but played with the shoulders instead of the feet.

They had annual ceremonies to ask blessing for the seeds they had planted. The priest would chant: "Mother of Noma, show favor to us. Let us suffer no famine; we call on you each year with our prayers. We have not forgotten you." There were also special dances to induce the spirit to grant them a plentiful crop.

The Borinquéns were a hospitable and friendly people as today's Puerto Ricans are still friendly and hospitable. Today's Puerto Ricans seem to have retained some of the old Indian ways. The tribes of the natives were mainly extended families. Today a man in Puerto Rico will still tell you he has 200 cousins: a kinship means relatives who will help in times of sickness or trouble. This is especially true among the poor, but extends to most of the people; Columbus wrote about "the guilelessness and generosity of these children of nature. They invite

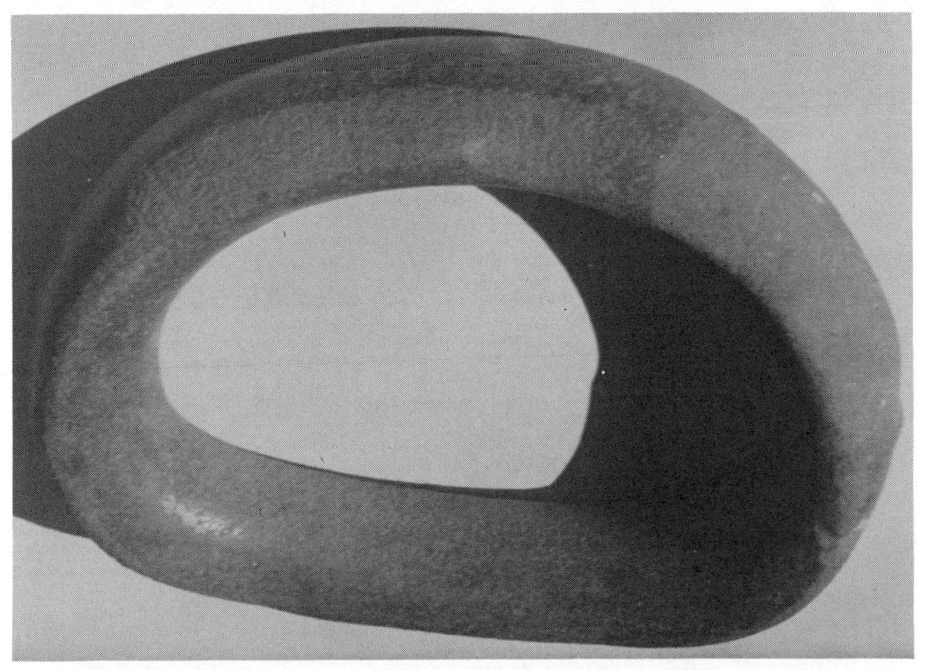

A ceremonial collar carved out of stone that was once worn by an Indian in the pre-Columbian era. (PHOTO COURTESY OF INSTITUTO DE CULTURA PUERTORIQUEÑA.)

Dominican monks accompanying Ponce de Leòn brought the Christian faith to the island. (PHOTO COURTESY OF PUERTO RICO TOURISM DEVELOPMENT.)

you to share anything they possess and show as much love as if their hearts went into it. . . . It is proven that amongst them the land belongs to everybody, just as does the sun or the water. . . . They seem to live in that golden world, wherein man lived simply and innocently . . . content only to satisfy nature."

There was said to be a 'King' of Borinquén and below him other "caciques" or chieftains. There were some feminine leaders in authority too, and the women were reputed to be most gifted in the arts of poetry and song.

Indian words have remained in the Borinquén's language; hamaca

The interior courtyard of the Dominican Convent still echoes with the peace that the Dominican Fathers sought when they built it in the sixteenth century. Now the building is the home of the Institute of Puerto Rican Culture, restored in 1966. (PHOTO COURTESY OF PUERTO RICO TOURISM DEVELOPMENT.)

(hammock), bohios (huts), huracán (hurricane), tabaco (tobacco), canoa (canoe). Many of the villages and towns still have Indian names, and usually were built on old Indian sites. Indians who fled from the Spaniards to hide in the hills were called "jibaro," meaning a free man in the Arawakan language. The rural countryman from the mountains is still called a "jibaro" and expresses an independence of spirit. The last drop of wine or liquor from a glass or cup will still be thrown on the ground as a sharing of the libation with the gods. An atavistic instinct going back for more than seven centuries.

Juan Ponce de Leon wrenched the natives from their old ways and customs, took from them their free peaceful lives, and turned them into virtual slaves, harshly treated. They were forced to work in the mines for the precious gold he wanted. He was officially appointed governor in March 1509, and was one of the islands harshest rulers. He almost decimated the Indians, by making them work exhausting hours in the mines, and through the cruelty he and his men perpetrated against them. Also, the Spanish had brought new diseases such as measles. The old herbal medicines were ineffective and thousands died in epidemics. The population dropped from its previous high level to that of a few thousand, though surprisingly, a record of 1787 shows there were still 2,300 full-blooded Indians in

Puerto Rico. These probably were mostly the "jibaros" who escaped to the hills and intermarried.

The Catholic Church was also to introduce its own means of subduing the natives. Dominican monks accompanying Ponce de Leon brought the Christian faith. The Spaniards said they had come to the New World "to find gold and save souls." Puerto Rico was the first island to which the Holy Inquisition was brought. This was directed by Bishop Alonso Manso, who was made General Inquisitor for the Indians and remained as Bishop of Puerto Rico for twenty-eight years. The Indians were forced to accept the invader's religion as they were forced to accept his language and his customs. In this, however, there was a unifying element which tied them and the culture of the island to that of the other islands of the Spanish Antilles and to the countries of Latin America: a tie that had existed through the centuries and still exists today.

The contrast between the island inhabitants of Boriquén and that of its invaders was so great that some historians suggest it was the Conquistadores who were the barbarians, not the people they vanquished.

2
The Spanish History

REBELLIONS against the Spaniards began early in 1511. The first was led by an Indian "cacique" Guarionex, with three thousand warriors. In the second battle led by Agueybana, there were fewer men. A third attempt to destroy the invaders was made by his son Agueybana II, who was able to muster several thousands of desperate Indians behind him.

Another was led by a cacique, Humacoa. This name is still kept by one of the present towns. There were also rebellions of Indians and blacks newly brought to the island. An Indian princess married to her Spanish lover—some Indians and Spaniards did fall in love—also led a revolt. But all were unsuccessful. The Spaniards were in Puerto Rico to stay for the next four hundred years.

Gold was in small supply in Puerto Rico, and soon news of seemingly inexhaustible amounts in Mexico sent the Spaniards in droves from the Greater Antilles. Spain had to issue an edict that a number of Spaniards must stay on the islands to colonize them. At first, Puerto Rico's governor was under the jurisdiction of Hispaniola by an "adelantado" sent by the Crown. Later, along with the other islands, it came under the wider jurisdiction of Mexico. By then the strategic value of Puerto Rico had been recognized, and lacking sufficient revenue of its own, it was given a yearly stipend to help in the expenses of building and maintaining its magnificent string of forts to form a haven against the mounting raids on the Spanish treasure fleets.

Meanwhile, since there were now insufficient Indians to work the mines and do the other labor on the islands, black slaves were imported. The first shipment of 4,000 slaves went to Hispaniola in 1517, to be re-distributed to Cuba and Puerto Rico. From this small beginning of 4,000, in the three islands, millions of black slaves were brought to the Spanish colonies, to the Caribbean islands that later came into other European hands, and to North America. The slave trade lasted three hundred and fifty years and was a great source of wealth to Spain, Britain, France, and North America.

From that early date of 1517, blacks began their contributions to the island by their labor, traditions, and culture which also goes into the making of present day Puerto Rico. They have particularly influenced the music of the island by the rhythm of their drums. In later times, many were prominent on the Puerto Rican scene. Their labor produced the wealth of the sugar and tobacco and coffee plantations on which the economy of the island rested for centuries.

They were people, as the Indians, upon whom an alien culture was imposed. People in this case speaking different tongues, but who could look back to civilizations of value in their own country of Africa. They came from Ghana, a thriving state renowned for its wealth in gold; from the intellectual center of Sudan, where the King was renowned for the splendor of his court; from Timbuktu, an important commercial, industrial, and intellectual center in the sixteenth century. Their background included the arts from Yoruba and Ife and Belin. Some came from more primitive places in the interior regions of Africa. When they landed, after surviving the hell of trade ships, they were treated as cruelly as the Indians had been. They became the new labor force. Where the number of Indians had been limited to the inhabitants, now there was an inexhaustible supply of blacks through the ever-growing slave trade that over the centuries grew into the millions in the New World.

Yet, relatively fewer blacks came to Puerto Rico than to the other islands and to North America. Though there were plantations, Puerto Rico was essentially centered around the garrison town of San Juan. A Captain-General was given full control in running the island. Also from time to time, new groups of garrison troops arrived on the island. There were also European and South American refugees, usually conservatives, who came to the island, as well as the French upper class who fled Haiti when it was taken over by the blacks. European pirates also intermarried with the islanders in the more remote parts of Puerto Rico and carried on a smuggling trade. In a later period, runaway slaves from islands that had been wrested from Spain's hands, were freed if they would accept the Catholic faith. So there were early groups of blacks on the island who were not slaves but free men.

Today in an enclave just outside of San Juan on the shore to the east are people who may have amongst their ancestors some of the very first blacks on the island. They still live in thatched roofed huts in a palm forest by the ocean. They fish, keep goats, chickens, and pigs, cultivate small plots as their forefathers did, and travel from there to their work. Their annual "fiesta" is so colorful that it has become one of the widest known on the island.

Except for a few women included on Columbus's third voyage, the Spaniards had brought no women with them. The Spaniards therefore took, mostly by rape, the Indian women. In 1514, because of the necessity of repopulating the country if a settlement was to be developed, a decree was issued allowing Spaniards to marry Indian women. Undoubtedly through these women, and the offspring whom the mothers would have in their care, remnants of the old Indian culture were kept alive. Also, the old people in the hills would have transmitted some of the Indian traditions.

With the influx of blacks from Africa, there was to be a further mixing. The Puerto Rican of today is a mestizo, a mixture by intermarriage of all three races. In many families, there may be black, light brown, and white-skinned children, who are brothers and sisters.

The Spaniards never had the same feelings in regard to mixed blood and mixed marriages as do the Anglo-Saxons. This may be because they themselves had been conquered and ruled by Moors for seven hundred years. Indeed the Moors added greatly to the Spanish culture, having a special influence on their architecture. It was not until the reign of King Ferdinand and Queen Isabella, who sponsored Christopher Columbus's voyages, that the Moors were driven from the country.

The Spaniards were now beginning to make their contribution to the island they had so senselessly wrecked. From Spain was brought sugar cane seeds, which grew well in the lush climate of the islands. With black labor, the plantations were organized and flourished. The Spaniards also brought horses. Most of these horses ran wild and multiplied quickly, so that Puerto Rico was able to send herds of them later to other islands, Peru, Mexico and Florida. The conquistadores also brought cattle, sheep, donkeys and chickens. Some of the ships coming to the "Indies" must have looked, in regard to their cargo, like Noah's Ark.

A King's Garden was set up in Puerto Rico, the first agricultural experimental station. Citrus fruits—oranges, lemons, and grapefruit, were introduced, as well as bananas brought from the Canaries and Algiers. Cereals, too, were introduced: barley, wheat, rice. Leather-

A portrait of Queen Isabella of Castile, who helped finance the discoveries of Christopher Columbus in the New World. (PHOTO COURTESY OF INSTITUTO DE CULTURA PUERTORRIQUEÑA.)

work became important using the hides of cows, pigs, and goats. The craft of ironwork was developed. The wheel, which was unknown to the Indians, came to the island too and so there was the making of ploughs, wagons, and carriages. The canoe of the Indian gave place to the sailing ships. Island woods were used for the new vessels, and shipbuilding was begun in neighboring Cuba. The "mestizos" were the craftsmen blending old styles of ornamentation into the new products. Towns were growing up over the island. Within an amazingly short while the Spanish had completely transformed the old Indian villages into Spanish colonial towns. The activity was intensive and varied.

Ponce de Leon had first started a settlement in San German. Here stands one of the oldest permanent religious buildings within the

A portrait of King Ferdinand, who by his marriage to Queen Isabella joined together two large sections of the country, thereby beginning the development of modern Spain in the fifteenth century. (PHOTO COURTESY OF INSTITUTO DE CULTURA PUERTO-RIQUEÑA.)

New World, Porta Coeli, built in 1606. There had been an earlier church built in 1512 but that was destroyed by the Indians. Religious buildings and forts were started early in San Juan. After finding that San German was not a suitable permanent base, Ponce de Leon moved to Caparra Heights, now a suburb of San Juan, and then to the present capital. For here was a large, almost landlocked harbor, ideal as a defensive position. Originally, the island was called San Juan (after St. John the Baptist) and the new capital was named Puerto Rico (rich port), but with time, the names were changed. San Juan was the second city to be built by the Conquistadores in 1508, (Santo Domingo had been started in 1494). But San Juan was the first city in the

San Juan was the first city in the hemisphere to be granted a coat of arms by the Spanish Crown on November 11, 1511.

hemisphere to be granted a coat of arms by the Spanish Crown on November 11, 1511.

The town was planned around a "plaza" or square as were all the towns on the island. On one side is usually the Alcadia or Mayor's office. In the case of San Juan, it was supposed to be a close replica of that in Madrid. Usually, on the other side of the square, the church was built. In San Juan the cathedral and churches were built with their own plazas. The Casa Blanca (White House) was erected for Ponce de Leon in 1521, and though he never lived in it, it passed on to his family and remained in their hands until 1773. By then, the first wooden structure had long been replaced, and it was then passed on to the Spanish military commanders.

Each town in Puerto Rico has its distinctive plaza reminiscent of old Spain. This one in Ponce, on the southern coast, is among the largest. Dominating the plaza are the twin towers of the Church of Nuestra Senora de (Our Lady of) Guadalupe. (PHOTO COURTESY OF PUERTO RICO INFORMATION SERVICE.)

Central Arecibo with church and plaza beside the Atlantic Ocean. (PHOTO BY FRANK H. WADSWORTH.)

The ornate iron gate marks the entrance to Casa Blanca (White House) begun by Ponce de Leòn in 1521 to be his home. He was killed before Casa Blanca was finished, but his descendants lived there for generations. Now the restored Casa Blanca contains a museum of early Puerto Rican life. (PHOTO COURTESY OF PUERTO RICO TOURISM DEVELOPMENT.)

By 1523, a convent was constructed for the Dominican Friars. As a counterpoint, three years later, a brothel was given a license, and houses of prostitution continued to be legal until well into the nineteenth century. Next to the Friars' convent, the Church of San José was built in 1532. San Juan Cathedral was started earlier as an edifice of thatch and wood, but by 1540, a proper stone building was erected. Here the remains of Ponce de Leon lie buried. He was wounded in a battle with Indians in Florida and then returned to Cuba, where he died. Later his bones were returned to Puerto Rico.

The architecture of the churches and cathedrals was naturally

Balcony overlooking San Juan Cathedral, where the remains of Ponce de Leòn, are buried. (PHOTO COURTESY OF PUERTO RICO INFORMATION SERVICES.)

similar to that of the same period in Spain. They were mostly Gothic in style with some admixture of Baroque and showed the Italian influences of the Renaissance. San Juan Cathedral has two very beautiful vaulted Gothic ceilings. Churches were built on a fairly large scale so that they might serve as places not only for worship but where large numbers of people might flee for safety in times of attacks upon the island. These early buildings were the first sites of European culture in the New World.

Then there began the serious and systematic building of forts to guard the town. There was La Fortaleza, with embattlements on the harbor. La Fortaleza is now the Governor's palace. The biggest project was the construction of El Morro Castle. Eighteen-foot thick walls were constructed, one hundred and forty feet above the water

El Morro, the military and architectural marvel, towers above the sea at the tip of Old San Juan. Begun in 1580s, the fort withstood a long series of attacks—including one by Sir Francis Drake. (PHOTO COURTESY OF PUERTO RICO TOURISM DEVELOPMENT.)

level at the headland jutting into the ocean. (The dungeons below later held many political prisoners—patriots who wanted independence for Puerto Rico. They were held captive as enemies of Spain). Ever new construction went into the immense fortress, Puerto Rico's

The incredible thickness of the walls of El Morro Fortress can be seen clearly from above. El Morro was the chief fortress in San Juan's defense system. (PHOTO COURTESY OF PUERTO RICO TOURISM DEVELOPMENT.)

Part of El Morro Fortress is seen in the background from a deep-sea fishing boat leaving San Juan Harbor for the ocean. (PHOTO COURTESY PUERTO RICO INFORMATION SERVICE.)

prime guardian against attack. Italian military architects were brought to the island, the finest planners of their time. Reinforcements and enlargements were carried out over three centuries. Two other forts were built around the town—San Cristobal and San Geronimo. Finally, a great wall was built around the city itself. A garrison was lodged in El Morro and most of the citizens lived within the town walls. San Juan is one of the only completely walled cities in the whole of the Americas.

The nonreligious buildings in the towns were constructed in Spanish-Moorish style then prevalent in Spain. They were built around courtyards and had tiled roofs and dark wooden balconies. Much of old San Juan today still retains the character of the Spanish colonial period.

The streets are laid out in straight lines from the central plaza, making continuing larger squares. There were probably about eighty houses in the original city of San Juan.

Yet none of these early European influences could be transported into so different a climate, nor overlay so different a culture without some modifications. The new generation of "mestizo" artisans who carried out the work introduced some measure of differences from the European models they copied.

In the countryside "haciendas" were built. These were the cotton, sugar, and coffee plantation homes of the Spaniards. In time, coffee became a gourmet export from Puerto Rico. Tobacco, an Indian product, was grown in ever larger quantities. Spaniards had learnt to smoke from the natives and found they enjoyed it. The habit spread to all Europe.

By the middle of the seventeenth century, some one hundred years after the capital and El Morro were started, the Spanish fleets laden with treasure put into San Juan for provisions. It became the winter port of the fleet and the gateway to and from Spain. The one great road built from the north to the south of the island was the Carretera Militar—the military road. Puerto Rico's strategic value was by then fully recognized. When the news spread through Europe of the Great Discovery and its great wealth, pirates, and buccaneers invaded the area and raided the Spanish ships. They chose islets and hidden coves on the island in which to bury their stolen treasure.

The scenes in Puerto Rico in the next century following the Conquest had completely changed from when the Spaniards first arrived. San Juan was one of the most important towns in the Caribbean.

The Caribbean islands of Puerto Rico, Hispaniola, and Cuba were very important at this time. It was their harbors from which ships sailed to and from all the countries of South America, Central America, and Spain. The islands were centers of communication—receiving information, passing on information, inciting rumors, and spreading gossip. There were many ships passing through the passages between the islands. They were the links between Spain and Latin America. The excitement that must have been generated at the sight of a ship from shore can be imagined. Is it a Spanish ship? Is it a pirate?

As more Spaniards arrived, more towns sprang up, and the population increased though slowly. The port towns were especially crowded when the fleets put in to stock up for the homeward journey. Cattle meat was salted and dried by the colonists to sell to the sailing ships. The ships' captains, dressed in large plumed hats, golden collars, breastplates, sashes, heavy gauntlets, and ribboned rosettes strolled the narrow streets. Their black hair was long; their beards were pointed; and their mustaches were twin handles of bristles on their faces. While the local gentry must have eagerly sought the latest news from them, the local ladies probably swooned over their virile, dashing appearances. They probably listened with the utmost admiration to stories of privateers fought and of battles won on the seas.

In the cities, the women were dressed gaily and the men handsomely Horse-drawn carriages clattered down the cobbled streets. The planters came from their "haciendas" in the country to be entertained in the great houses. This was the place to hear the latest news and gossip from Europe and South America.

The scene from the 'bateyes' to the plazas had completely changed. Men and women no longer walked around almost naked except for headbands, golden ornaments, and perhaps a brief colored cloth. Now everyone was fully clothed. The Spanish men wore their elegant European styles. Their wives and women wore long dresses, twirled parasols, and flicked fans. The native Indian men now wore pantaloons and loose shirts. The Indian women wore petticoats and loose shifts. Often the Indian women were dressed by their mistresses, in the peasant costumes of various regions of Spain such as Andalusia. By edict of the viceroy, they were commanded to part their hair in the center. The blacks provided bright color with kerchiefs and full skirts. The house servants were usually dressed in hand-me-downs of their masters and mistresses. The priests and monks passed in their long brown or black robes from the church to the monastery. Even the children were in some way clad, except for shoes. For centuries, shoes were the possessions of the privileged.

There was ringing of iron being beaten at the blacksmiths for horseshoes. At open stores one could see leather work being done or elaborate grill work being created for the houses. There was the constant sound of hammering and construction as new buildings were being constructed. There was a vigorous sense of purpose in the air, as the cities were being built.

Spain was at the height of its power and expanding its empire. This was reflected in the colonies. What was happening in Spain was always reflected in the islands. Later when Spain was in decline, the early vigor and excitement would fall into dullness and apathy.

These cities in the islands, were built one hundred years before any cities appeared in North America. As Professor Gordon Lewis has said, "The Caribbean is a region of great antiquity and a rich and brilliant heritage."

In the early sixteenth century, the Spanish Crown had formed a "Casa de la Contraction" to organize and supervise the ships sailing between the Indies. In Puerto Rico, no commercial ships were allowed except from Seville to San Juan. With such limitations, smuggling became an important business. In 1644, there was not a single store in San Juan, by then a town of forty-five hundred inhabitants, that did not engage in the smuggling trade. Though it was against Spanish law, the town bartered its animals, hides, lumber, fruits, and grain in return for clothing and other manufactured articles which the French, English, and Dutch traded. Not until 1800 did Spain allow free commerce with the British colonies of North America and not until 1815, free commerce with other nations.

Smuggling was as much a way of life on all the islands as fighting pirates. Smugglers of all European nationalities had their special coves and enclaves throughout the Caribbean. To safeguard the vast treasure Spain received from South America, Spain was forced to adopt the Venetian fleet system, since individual ships sailing alone had become too vulnerable against the activities of privateers or Sea-Beggers.

In 1554, a French captain with ten ships menaced the islands before capturing Santiago and Cuba. In 1555, a Frenchman with only two ships captured Havana, razed it, and withdrew to sea again within three weeks.

Sir John Hawkins, an English merchant and sea captain, was the first of the English interlopers. He set out more for trade than piracy. He brought goods from England and slaves from Africa and traded them for gold and hides. Queen Elizabeth was delighted with his excellent returns and contributed ships for further voyages. Many of the Spanish colonists were prepared to do business with him.

Sir Henry Morgan had been kidnapped as a child in Bristol and sold as an indentured servant in Barbados. He later ran off to become

San Juan was first unsuccessfully attacked by Sir Francis Drake in 1592. (PHOTO COURTESY INSTITUTO DE CULTURA PUERTORRIQUEÑA.)

a buccanneer. When the British were lacking sufficient ships and armies to fight in the West Indies, they used the buccanneers as their mercenaries. Morgan was so successful that he was later appointed lieutenant governor of Jamaica for his services to England in fighting the Spanish enemy on the High Seas. By this time, the North American colonies became involved in the smuggling trade. In the late seventeenth century the New England ports were the best

Queen Elizabeth the First of England, who wanted Puerto Rico as an English colony and sent Sir Francis Drake and the Earl of Cumberland to do her bidding. (PHOTO COURTESY INSTITUTO DE CULTURA PUERTORRIQUEÑA.)

markets for stolen cargoes. They continued to be so into the eighteenth century. New England consciences had no difficulty in coming to profitable terms with cutthroat buccanneers.

The Hapsburg ambitions had strained Spain's resources to the breaking point. Taxation, an adverse trade balance, and unwise economic decisions added to Spain's difficulties. Portugal and Catalonia revolted. The Portuguese regained their independence. Spain continued to war with France. All this added to the general decay and decline of Spanish power. Spain was able to retain most of her American empire—Florida, Mexico, nearly all Central America, and South America (except for Brazil). Within a few years of Spain's occupation of Latin America, the Portuguese had settled in and claimed that country.

Spain had also kept the most important Caribbean islands: Cuba, Puerto Rico, and two-thirds of Hispaniola. The French had by this time encroached on the other third.

More and more other European countries entered into the Caribbean, fought in its waters, and challenged or captured some of Spain's territories in the New World. By 1634, Curaçao was already in the hands of the Dutch. Jamaica, which was discovered by Columbus in 1494, was captured by the English in 1655. The west side of Hispaniola, later renamed Haiti, was by 1697 in the hands of the French.

Havana had been thought to be impregnable but it fell to the British in 1762. The British destroyed part of the Spanish naval force and opened the port to world trade. After the war, England gave Cuba back to Spain in return for Florida.

The year 1801 found Great Britain supreme in the Caribbean, with the French confined to Guadaloupe, and the Spaniards to Cuba and Puerto Rico; the whole island of Hispaniola being then in the hands of Toussaint L'Ouverture, the Haitian general and a principal leader of the slave insurrection.

Britain was so anxious to possess Puerto Rico that she attacked three times.

San Juan was first unsuccessfully attacked by Sir Francis Drake in 1595. (This was after he had defeated the Spanish Armada in the English Channel.) To prevent his landing, two vessels were sunk in San Juan harbor to block the entrance. The cannons from El Morro then blasted at the English fleet. Drake withdrew but tried again to effect a landing the next day. He lost nine ships during the engagement and finally left. Drake's aim had been to seize gold being stored in La Fortaleza. Drake did capture the town of Santo Domingo on the neighboring island, and held it for a month until he was given a ransom of twenty-five thousand "pieces of eight." In 1598, three years later, Queen Elizabeth I of England outfitted a fleet of eighteen ships, under the command of the Earl of Cumberland, with orders to turn Puerto Rico into an English colony. Gaining experience from his predecessor's mistake in adopting a frontal attack, Cumberland approached the city from the land side. Ignominiously, he fell into the water from a bridge and almost drowned. However, he captured the town, and held it for about five months. An epidemic of dysentery among Cumberland's forces finally vanquished the English, and they

A drawing of the Earl of Cumberland showing him in full armor. In the background his fleet is anchored in the harbor of San Juan, which he captured and held for a short time in 1598. (PHOTO COURTESY OF INSTITUTO DE CULTURA PUERTORRIQUEÑA.)

had to retire. Before leaving they burned and looted the town. Part of their booty included the bells of the Cathedral and a considerable amount of sugar and hides, but no gold.

The next attempt on the city, in 1626, was made by the Dutch. They managed to sail right into San Juan harbor. The Spanish opened fire from El Cañuelo on the other side of the bay, as well as from the cannons of El Morro. Caught between the two, the Dutch retreated. However, they too set fire to the town before leaving.

Except for a small fray by two British boats in 1702 and another unsuccessful British attack in 1795, in Arecibo, the island remained quiet and impregnable for many years. The last attack was under the command of General Ralph Abercromby who tried to land with seven thousand. The battle lasted for over two months when the British withdrew from its final effort to take Puerto Rico by force. San Juan remained in Spanish hands, protected by its complex of fortresses, which continued to be enlarged and reinforced. El Morro stood as a sentinel, hurling back all would-be invaders.

The series of fortresses still stand, impressive to view today. The U.S. Army until recently, operated a base from Fort Brooke at the entrance of the castle.

Politics in Europe were a major factor in Caribbean history. This area was often the most important center of wars and clashes between the powers who changed sides as they changed alliances during the seventeenth, eighteenth, and nineteenth centuries. Many of the smaller islands were captured and held, recaptured and reheld by the rival powers. St. Croix, for instance, came under the domination of France, Spain, England, Denmark, and Holland until it was purchased by the United States from the Dutch in 1917.

Puerto Rico and her sister islands of San Domingo (once Hispaniola) and Cuba, as well as the vast continent of Latin America, remained in Spain's hands and were part of her empire until the Wars of Independence (The Spanish American Revolution led by Simon Bolívar from 1808 to 1826) at the beginning of the 19th century. That was when most of her empire was lost. Puerto Rico and Cuba remained in Spanish hands until 1898, four hundred years after Columbus's discovery.

3

The Early Structuring of Puerto Rican Society

THE Indians had burnt the Spanish towns and destroyed the whole of the South and Southwest to force the Spaniards from their shores. The Spaniards had brought supplies with them by sea. The Indians suffered from hunger, disease, and enforced labor. It was soon realized that while the Indians were working in the mines, there was no one to tend the fields. The Spaniards had not come to the New World for such hard work. In this, they contrasted with the Pilgrims who came to New England.

As it became necessary to start growing food on the island, Indians belonging to the Crown, and those whose owners had died, were given their freedom so that they could once again till the fields. It was they and their children, the new generation of mestizos, from Indian mother and Spanish father who put the old traditional skills back into use. This was particularly so in the growing of yams, yucca, cassava, and maize (the wheat the Spaniards brought never did well), the retending of the fruit trees, and the cultivation of tobacco. As the earth revived, and the fields were beginning to flourish once more, it was the newly arrived slaves from Africa who labored in them. This was particularly true in the cane fields. The cane seeds of sugar that the Spaniards had brought over did well in the lush soil of the tropics. But it demanded much grueling labor.

The first sugar mill started in Puerto Rico was in 1523, eight years after the first introduction of slaves. As the years went by sugar mills

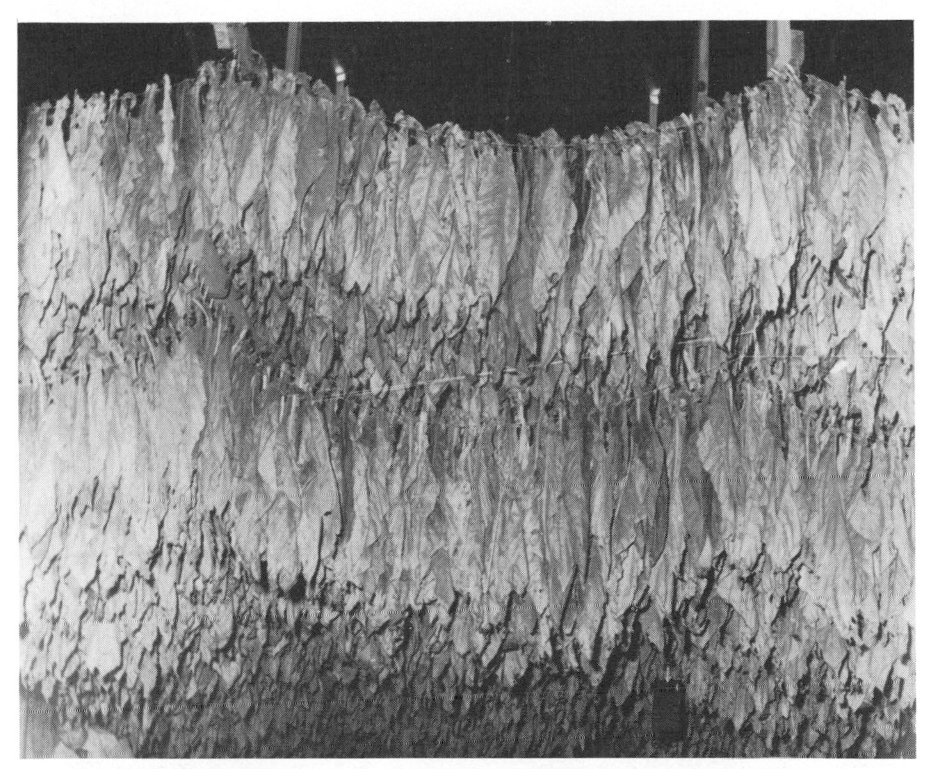

Tobacco plants being dried and cured before being sent to factories to be made into cigars. (PHOTO COURTESY OF U.S. DEPARTMENT OF AGRICULTURE.)

were established. Overseers from the Canary Islands, who were familiar with the growing and processing of the cane, were brought over. More slaves were brought, too, as the number of plantations increased. Spain did not engage directly in the slave trade. At first the supply of slaves was furnished by the Portuguese. Later the contract for supplying the colonies with slaves was given to Great Britain by the treaty of Urecht.

As the slaves landed they were branded like cattle with a hot iron bearing the royal seal. This habit of branding slaves was not discontinued until 1784.

"Day after searing day, week after week, year after tortured year, the slaves toiled and died." More and more slaves had to be brought in. Slavery did not end in Puerto Rico until 1873. The following is a description by a Puerto Rican author, Manuel Maldonado-Denis, of the slave's condition in Puerto Rico a century before emancipation:

The coarse cloth which covers part of his bare body neither defends him from the heat of day nor the harmful night dew: the food that is given him—cassava, sweet potatoes, bananas and such things—

Her ancestors probably came to Puerto Rico in the early sixteenth century, when the first slaves were brought to the island. (PHOTO COURTESY OF PUERTO RICO TOURISM DEVELOPMENT.)

> scarcely suffices to sustain his wretched existence; deprived of everything he is condemned to continuous labor, always subject to experiencing the cruelty of his greedy and fierce master. . . . A white insults any of them with impunity and in the most contemptible terms; some masters treat them with despicable harshness; getting pleasure out of keeping the tyrant's rod always raised and thereby causing disloyalty, desertion, and suicide.

Sometimes the slaves were allowed small pieces of land, which in their infrequent periods of not working on the plantations, they could cultivate for themselves. Even after eighteen hours in the fields, they did manage to cultivate their tiny lots.

In his history of black slavery *Historia de La Esclavirtud Negra Puerto Rico,* written in 1865 Luis Diaz Solers points out that under the law, slave owners were supposed to give some small piece of land to their slaves. Here they grew a variety of crops, vegetables, and fruits. They raised a few chickens, a pig or a goat, not only to help sustain themselves but to save a few pesos towards eventual freedom.

In the nineteenth century, Puerto Rico had a severe monetary problem. Taxes were paid and land was bought with coffee, cotton, or rice. In this situation, slaves who had saved some money were able to lend it out at interest which accumulated over the years. The slaves' frugal savings, interestingly, sometimes helped in providing funds for small merchants' businesses. The slave then used the money to buy freedom. Ex-slaves living near San Juan were also given plots of land and supplies to build cabins. In return, they had to help mount the guns of the forts.

How the blacks were treated depended on the disposition of their masters. One elderly lady in Puerto Rico, in a recent newspaper interview, related how liberal her family had been in the nineteenth century. She illustrated this fact by saying that the house slaves did not need to kneel before speaking to their masters.

The importation of blacks was less, and the intermingling of blacks and natives was freer in Puerto Rico than in the other Caribbean islands. By law the slave was considered to be a person and not a chattel as another piece of property of the master. In practice, however, what Spain decreed was not necessarily followed in the faraway colony. During times of sugar booms, when there was much money to be made from sugar, the slave tended to be worked harder than usual and treated more harshly. There was some relaxation, however, during other periods.

After the initial excitement of exploration, development, and battle, a sense of quiet settled over Puerto Rico. The foreign attacks which had spelled danger to the island had stopped. The Spanish fleet was using Havana more than San Juan, which took second place. There was a long period of uninterrupted peace making possible a life of easy leisure for the military and the ruling classes. The governors, the garrison officers, and the plantation owners led a social life filled with days and nights of playing cards, gambling, and dancing at elaborate balls. (Playing cards were in such demand that they were sold by the Treasury as a source of revenue.) The Spanish soldiery, though miserably paid, had plenty of time for carousing and making love to the beautiful Creole girls. Many of these Creoles

In the mountains water is never lacking. It has been this way for centuries. (PHOTO BY FRANK H. WADSWORTH.)

helped to support the soldiers by giving them food.

Spain allowed no island trade or commerce except with herself. As we have already stated, this led inevitably to smuggling as a way of life. The islanders were almost forced to barter goods from the new neighboring French, British and Dutch islands, even though these were old, and sometimes current, enemies. It was so much cheaper and easier to engage in this illegal commerce than to obtain many costlier goods from faraway Spain. Coffee, remember, had become a gourmet export. Soon it was flourishing on Puerto Rican hillsides and mountainsides. This product were marketable through legitimate trade with Spain. But there were many day-to-day essentials which were better sold closer to home. Cattle and horses which had multiplied were sold. Envoys came even from Florida and Peru to obtain them. There were "wild" men in the interior, somewhat like American cowboys, who rode horses to round up the wild cattle. Food, especially good vegetables, was now plentiful on the island and there was enough for exchange.

The American colonies were taking part in the contraband trade: a three-way trade in molasses, rum, and slaves. Respectable New Englanders were not averse to making a great deal of money in this way. Puerto Rican merchants were not averse on their part for profitable dealings. We can see why commerce between North

America and Puerto Rico began a long time ago. When in the early nineteenth century, Spain was forced to reform her trading laws by allowing the colonies to have other trading partners than herself, the movement of ships between the islands and the United States begun long before, increased considerably.

Naturally Spain frowned on the contraband activities of her subjects. The garrison was costing Spain revenue acquired from her Mexican colonies and she was receiving little back in the way of taxes.

In 1765, she sent an Irishman, Field Marshal Alejandro O'Reilly, to make a study of the island. He found those responsible for the community given over to a life of pleasure; the production of crops far below their potential; the smuggling and illegal trading hardly hidden. He made several suggestions: an increase in the quota of sugar the island should produce; new colonists should be sent from Spain and given land, especially artisans and farmers; rigid trade laws be liberialized; Puerto Rico put on a self-sustaining basis. He also took a census of the island population. He had a very disdainful attitude towards the mixed population. Further, he organized an infantry company of black slaves who were to take part in the defense of San Juan in 1797. San Juan was declared "A Defence of the First Order."

O'Reilly was born in Dublin, and grew up to be a soldier of fortune. He joined the Spanish army while he was still a youth. Later he fought both for France and Austria. Returning to Spain, his military talents were recognized by Charles III and he was made governor of Madrid. Then he was sent over to the colonies to obtain up-to-date information about them for the monarch. Though he spent only forty-five days in Puerto Rico, he was responsible for a number of changes including those already mentioned and considerable new construction work being done on the old fortresses. O'Reilly wrote warmly of the land, if not in quite so glowing terms as Columbus.

"It is bathed by copious rivers which abound in good fish; in the mountains, water is never lacking; there are fertile and bountiful plains, and two or even three harvests of corn, rice and other crops are raised every year." He spoke of cotton, indigo, coffee, pepper, cacoa, nutmeg and vanilla; of timber for furniture in the mountains, of countless medicinal roots and herbs. And of the sugar cane, he wrote, it is "the thickest, tallest, juiciest and sweetest in America."

Puerto Rican society in the seventeenth and eighteenth century could be compared to the form of a pyramid. At the top was the autocratic governor, considering himself a surrogate for the Crown, and with little except direct orders from Spain to restrain him. Most governors, therefore, were despots—little Caesars, little tyrants.

According to Manuel Maldonado-Denis citing Brother Inigo

Painting by José Campeche of the Spanish Governor Uztaria in the 18th century. Note the street scene of Old San Juan in the background. All power resided in the office of the governor. (PHOTO COURTESY OF INSTITUTO DE CULTURA PUERTORRIQUEÑA.)

Abbad, the first historian of Puerto Rico writing in 1796, the economic and political frameworks of Puerto Rico were the same: with the economy revolving around sugar cane, cotton, tobacco, and coffee. All power resided in the governor of the islands "from whom came all the orders, as the military and political governor, and as superintendent of the branches of the public treasury and the royal vice-patronate. He may intervene in the affairs of parishes, in the accounts of personal income, factories and churches; he disposes of

The officers of the garrison served a term of duty and then returned to Spain. A sergeant in the militia's infantry of Puerto Rico displaying the uniform worn in the 18th century in the Spanish army. (PHOTO COURTESY OF INSTITUTO DE CULTURA PUERTORRIQUEÑA.)

troops and militia for defense, reviews them, arbitrates their disputes, presides over the commissioners of the public treasury, and is the superior judge over all justices on the island." Under him were his entourage and those delegated by him to act as his administrators. Next came the officers of the garrison, who served a term of duty and then returned to Spain. Mixing with them socially were the plantation owners, who used overseers to carry out the functioning of their estates, and were interested only in the revenue which enabled them

According to the American chronicler who took this photograph in 1898, this group of Puerto Ricans was directly descended from the Tainos, who had intermarried with blacks to some extent.

and their families to live a life of pleasure. Below this group came the middle class of lawyers, doctors, importers, and exporters carrying on both legal and illegal commerce.

This whole group were mestizos. They belonged entirely to the island and did not go on occasional trips to Spain or Europe as the upper group did. In the next century when there would be changes, many of their sons and grandsons would go to Spain for their education, or as representatives in the Cortéz. But at this time, they were insulated and insular. Below them came the small farmers, artisans, and the shopkeepers. Still lower were the soldiery and the smugglers, many of whom had been common soldiers and sailors. The hazards of their new calling, despite the danger of being captured or being killed, offered a prospect of some riches. They lived in isolated coastal areas, marrying or living with local women. Some of them were of other nationalities, so there might occur blue-eyed, fair-haired children among their offspring.

The "campesinos" of the mountains were individualistic, whose forbears were Indians and blacks who had run away to escape one form or another of slavery. They were and still are the poor of the hills, who remain individualistic and retain the tradition of a free laborers' "dignidad."

Then there were the "free" blacks, and poorer mestizos. They had to carry with them a card showing where they were working. If they did not possess one, it was necessary quickly to obtain one, or they were in trouble. At the bottom base were the blacks kept in perpetual slavery. The former were not much better off than the latter, but they tended to do the somewhat easier work in the shade on the coffee plantations (coffee grows best in the shade of bigger trees), while the slaves did the grueling work in the burning sun.

The Church could be said to be the cement that kept the layers of the pyramid firmly in their proper places. Puerto Rico was then basically a clerico-military state. The first monks had come with the Conquistadors and built their convents and churches. The first to arrive were the Dominicans. The Franciscan monks came later in 1642 and began the erection of their own church and monastery. Many of them were Portuguese, and were not fully trusted by the Spanish authorities.

The Church functioned in the sphere of teaching as well as the saving of souls. This attractive, modern Church of Santa Maria Reina is on the campus of the Catholic University in Ponce. (PHOTO COURTESY OF PUERTO RICO INFORMATION SERVICE.)

The Church had its own pyramidal order and divergencies from the Bishops to the village priests. The priests and monks functioned in other spheres as well as the saving of souls. They were teachers, starting the first schools. They formed the Colegio de San Tomás de Aquino and the monasterio de San Francisco, which had the status of universities, the first in the Western Hemisphere long before Harvard and Yale. However, little more than theology and philosophy were taught.

They were also dispensers of charity. A Royal Hospital established in 1766 was actually an extension of an earlier military hospital. The local Bishop established a Civil Hospital with 500 beds and also established a smaller one for the poor. They thus served the entire community.

At the same time, they were controllers of immigration, seeing that no Jews or Protestants entered Puerto Rico. They were controllers of customs and censors of any literature arriving from abroad. Mostly they kept the intellectual lid on the island, reinforcing its insularity. They also went hand in hand with the authoritarianism of the military regime.

Going regularly to Mass and attending all other special religious services was obligatory for rich and poor. (It was easy in a small

The people were deeply and sincerely religious. The interior of the Museum of Religious Art in San German demonstrates the beauty and peace of this former church. Porta Coeli was a seventeenth-century chapel and was restored by the Institute of Puerto Rican Culture as a museum. (PHOTO COURTESY OF PUERTO RICO TOURISM DEVELOPMENT.)

community for priests to seek out delinquents and issue penances.) Attendance at these functions was probably a diversion for the poor from their everyday labors and an opportunity to show off new fashions for the ladies of society. However, the people were deeply and sincerely religious, devoted to the Catholic Church. From childhood they were strictly brought up in its precepts. They honored the Virgin Mary. No young girl of marriageable age was allowed out without a "duenna" in society circles. Whatever the indulgences of the men, the young women had to be virgins at marriage. They were closely and strictly guarded until they found husbands. Then the husbands took care of their guardianship. Legal prostitution helped to keep marriage "sacred." The poor were taught to be humble and not resent their God-ordained place in life.

Professor Robert D. Crassweller says that the Spanish love of authority, evinced by their devotion to church and the military and their love of anarchy, evinced by smuggling and evasion of the law, cohabited in peace. A Spaniard's idealism easily led him to believe that there was less disparity between theory and practice than he would have approved in principal. Today, Puerto Ricans still tend to break the laws and ordinances where they feel nobody minds and everybody does the same. They do not easily then turn into little bureaucrats when given a little authority. Again according to Professor Crassweller, there is "The personal and chaotic quality of public life"; as against "the warmth and devotion and loyalty that infuse the relationship of the individual with the family and with the select circle of friends who are drawn into the family."

This trait extended from the Indian tribe, which was composed of the larger family relations and kinship, and continued throughout the whole period of Puerto Rico's history, into the present day.

While some atavistic roots went back to the Indian and African forebears, it was the Spanish presence over the centuries that predominantly colored and shaped the people of Puerto Rico. Though later, because of historical and geographical differences, social differences of the mestizo and the Spaniard, political and economic reasons, the Puerto Ricans clearly showed a desire for a break-away from Spain.

In commemoration of Ferdinand VI's coming to the Spanish throne in 1746, Puerto Rico received its first minted coins of gold and silver. The name *Puerto Rico* was stamped on them. Fifty years later paper money was introduced for the first time as well as copper money. Puerto Rico's monetary system today is exactly the same as that of the United States.

The old evil god Huracan plagued the island from time to time causing devastation to the crops and flimsily built houses. Earthquake tremors were rare but one in May 1787 caused extensive damage even affecting some of the forts in San Juan. Pirates were still infesting the seas of the Caribbean, choosing islets and hidden coves on the island in which to bury their stolen treasure. This is depicted in Robert Louis Stevenson's Treasure Island, which is supposed to be set on an islet off Puerto Rico's southern shore. It is called "Caja de Meurta" (Dead Man's Chest). Other islands lay claim to the site of the story. Piracy continued well into the nineteenth century, so it was part of the local scene for over two hundred years. It has led to the writing of many romantic, swashbuckling tales.

There was one Puerto Rican pirate named Cofresi, who acted as sort of a Robin Hood of the seas. The treasure he captured from the Spanish and other ships, he gave to the Puerto Rican poor. Mona Island was one of his places of refuge, as it was for many pirates, buccaneers and smugglers. This island was an excellent place to obtain fresh water and good vegetables or to catch and roast a wild pig. Cofresi was finally captured (his boat being fired on and sunk by an American ship) in 1824 when he was only thirty-three years old. He had been a pirate for fifteen years. After capture, he was taken to El Morro Castle and executed. To the poor in Puerto Rico he had

Members of the Areyto Folkloric Ballet of Puerto Rico perform the "plena" as part of the LeLoLai celebration. The Areyto company's repertoire includes dances from all the different cultures that have contributed to modern day Puerto Rico. (PHOTO COURTESY OF PUERTO RICO TOURISM DEVELOPMENT.)

been a hero and he is still remembered in the island's legends.

During the seventeenth century, Puerto Rico was an isolated and sparsely populated island: the population by 1673 being only about two thousand. O'Reilly's census of 1765 showed that the total population had grown in a hundred years to 44,883. From that time on, it quickened rapidly, so that in the next hundred years it doubled with the number of towns now thirty-four and an equal number of churches. By the end of the eighteenth century the population had reached 150,000. By the end of the nineteenth century, it was to be a million.

The roughly 100,000 population figure of the census in 1787 was made up of about 2,000 purebred Indians, an almost equal number of whites and mulattos of over 40,000 each, and 15,000 blacks. It was mainly the mulattos whose families had now spent generations on the island who were beginning to differentiate themselves from the whites. The whites were Spaniards, whose homeland was Spain, who were termed the "peninsulares" or those from the peninsular.

With the increase in population, agricultural activity also greatly increased. There was a variety of crops. Coffee was predominant. Other crops included sugar, tobacco, cotton, citrus fruits, bananas (a dozen different varities), plantains, breadfruit, pineapples, mangoes, root vegetables, rice, and beans. These are now the staple food of Puerto Ricans.

The small farms of the peasants grew in numbers. An emissary to the island fifty years after O'Reilly, wrote: "A few coffee trees and plantains (a sort of large banana which is cooked while it is still green), a cow, a horse, and an acre of land in corn and sweet potatoes, constitute the property of what would be denominated a comfortable *jibaro*. This individual mounted on his emaciated horse, dressed in a broad-brimmed straw hat, cotton jacket, clean shirt and checkered pantaloons, sallies forth from his cabin to Mass, to a cockfight or a dance, thinking himself the most independent and happy being in existence."

Another description of Puerto Rico between the years 1745 to 1748 can be seen in an old manuscript in the United States Library of Congress. It is part of a captured English sailor's journal.

> "It is one of the finest islands I ever saw, and I verily believe not any one island of the West Indies is more capable of improvement than this; but through pride and sloth of the inhabitants it is the far greater part of it still a wilderness. It abounds in oranges, lemons, citrous limes, etc., in such plenty that they are not worth gathering. There are prodigious quantities of bananas, plantains, coco nutts, pine apples, mountain cabbage; with a great many other fruit and

Pineapples grow from long spiky leaves in rows along the ground and have always been plentiful. (PHOTO COURTESY U.S. DEPARTMENT OF AGRICULTURE.)

Breadfruit, gift from the South Pacific, is plentiful, and has been grown on the island for hundreds of years. (PHOTO BY FRANK H. WADSWORTH.)

vegetables—In short, there is not anything for the support of human nature but may here be found or cultivated. It might in the hands of the English and Dutch be rendered a paradise on earth, but the present inhabitants are mere devils."

From the Indians onwards, the islanders had always been warm and hospitable to strangers. It is difficult to imagine why the English sailor considered the people of Puerto Rico in the eighteenth century "mere devils." Perhaps he was harshly treated by the Spanish officers and soldiers. Perhaps, too, like later journalists, he was expressing a view he felt would please the authorities—in this case the British, enemies of Spain. Perhaps he was shocked by what he considered an apparent lack of industry. The small farmer, described earlier, who was content without any drive for further gains and wealth, was foreign to Anglo-Saxon standards.

The great growth in the population had a further effect upon society. The pyramid still stood but it was a far larger pyramid. The middle classes especially had increased. It was the men of this group who were to break out of the cocoon in which the island seemed to have slumbered so long. They wished less restrictiveness in trade. They wanted lifted such unpopular decrees as the prohibition of

A banana plantation, and in the background, as everywhere in Puerto Rico, are the mountains. (PHOTO COURTESY OF DEPARTMENT OF AGRICULTURE.)

making rum in Puerto Rico because it interfered with the sale of wines from Spain. They wanted greater contact with the outside world. They were still loyal to the Crown. Indeed, after the defeat of the English under Abercromby in 1795, the Spanish King had issued a declaration calling Puerto Ricans his "faithful and loyal subjects." But now they faced the mother country in a new spirit with new feelings and new ideas. They wanted some representation in government and more freedom in the conducting of their own affairs. Writings of the Enlightenment had been translated and printed in Mexico and smuggled into the island. They could not but have heard of the breakaway of the colonies of North America from England. However, the news of the French Revolution reverberated across the sea. The revolt of the slaves in Haiti had a direct effect upon Puerto Rico. The Haitien slaves had burnt all Haitian sugar fields. This resulted in a greater demand from Puerto Rico. The ensuing sugar boom brought greater prosperity to the island. French upper-class fled Haiti to the safety of Puerto Rico, and most stayed and made it their home. Another influx was to come a little later when the South American countries claimed their independence from Spain. Loyalists from South America also took refuge on the island.

The events in Spain itself had their effect upon and their reflections in Puerto Rico. Under Charles V, elected emperor in 1519 and his son Philip II, Spain was at the peak of its power, holding an enormous empire in the New World, claiming Naples and Milan as dependencies, holding sway over Austria and the Netherlands. However, from the time of the defeat of the Armada in 1588, Spain's power began to decline. In the War of Succession between 1700 to 1713, Spain lost all her European possessions. In the soon-to-begin Peninsular War from 1808 to 1814, Spain was herself occupied by French troops. During these wars, Puerto Rico got little help from the mother country.

Puerto Rico approached the new century in a new spirit, a new frame of mind. This was no longer a sparsely populated, somnolent outpost of empire. It was a flourishing island with a large number of people—a people beginning to think of themselves as a separate nation, with its own identity, an identity which had been evolving over the centuries.

When Ramón Power was elected to represent Puerto Rico in the Spanish Cortes in 1810 he did so as a Puerto Rican. He was first person to distinguish himself in this manner and the first to obtain some measures of reform for his countrymen. Other similar-minded men were to follow him.

Puerto Ricans were to face Spain in a fresh role in the coming decades. Puerto Rico could be said to have gone through a long period of gestation during which her Indian heritage, her African influences, and her Spanish culture had now given birth to a new nation to which her sons and daughters were proud to belong.

4
Puerto Rican Culture

A TRULY Puerto Rican culture did not flower until the beginning of the nineteenth century. It occurred concurrently with a flowering of patriotism. Puerto Rico became aware of itself as a separate nation from Spain. Spain was no longer the motherland, three thousand miles away, but the island itself. It was hills, mountains, forests, valleys, rivers, foliage, tropical flowers, and birds. It was its unique little tree frog, the "coquí," whose repetitive sounds filled the night air. It was its brilliant humming birds, its skies of a special blue, its beaches and the bright ocean surrounding them. It was the flaming orange arches of its flamboyant trees in summer along its country roads; its 'tulip' trees high and colorful most of the year; the palms that swayed in a magical dance in the trade winds; the sensuous shapes of banana trees; the flowering cane moving softly in the breezes, the red berries of the ripe coffee. This was truly an island of enchantment. This was not Spain. This was theirs—their own country. Spain was part of Europe. They were part of the Caribbean. The forces that shaped one were not the same forces that had shaped the other. As we have said at the ending of Chapter Three, the earlier centuries had been a period of gestation, during which had occurred a melding of the native Indians, the Spanish, and the African. This melding had created a people, a nation with a rich heritage. This heritage was the sum of the differing influences that had formed them. All the cultured expressions that followed were a result of this new sense of "puertorequeñismo." It has flourished ever since, and provided a developing and rigorous culture which has survived the later imposition of American culture.

A printing press had been set up in Mexico in 1535, soon after the Conquest. From Mexico came descriptive essays of the times by Fray Bartolomé de Las Casas, by Cabeza de Vaca, by Bernal Diaz del Castillo, and by Diego Velaquez and others. As well as descriptions of what was happening to the islands in their development, stories were being told. Some of these stories were old legends taken from the Indians, as well as some stories borrowed from Spain. Later the work of Creole writers and poets from South America found their way to the island. Even today, Latin American writers find a ready audience in the Spanish Antilles while writings from the islands by islanders were well-received in Mexico and South America. There was a bond of language and heritage among them.

All the early composers and poets and writers were patriots, whose theme was the liberation of their country; or they were creators of romantic songs and lyric poems and tales showing love of the land itself—poems to the beauty of Puerto Rico.

One of the most loved songs in Puerto Rico is one that speaks of "my exquisite Borica."

> You are called Preciosa by the waves of
> the sea that bathes you.
> Preciosa, because you are an enchantment,
> an ideal.
> You have the noble chivalry of Mother Spain,
> As well as the fiery song of the Indian brave.

A long list of poets and writers who are now revered, were, in one way or another, patriots. Those who became exiles for their political beliefs (usually choosing New York as their place of exile) wrote with special nostalgia of their island.

This literature, concerned with "puertoriqueñismo" began with a book published in 1849 by Dr. Manuel Alonso, a physician, who wrote *El Jibaro* which was a series of sketches about the life of the peasant of his time. His work was part of a literary movement that reflected concern with the island. Coll y Toste, a historian as well as a poet, was also a doctor of medicine. Again this was not unusual. Puerto Rico has its Chekhovs. Toste's famous *Boletin* comprises fourteen volumes. Also Tomas Blanco wrote "Pronturario Histoico de Puerto Rico." Another physician who was also a novelist, journalist, essayist, and patriot was Manuel Zeno Gandia. Dr. Ramon E. Betances, also a practicing physican, wrote an *Independence Manifesto* as well as a romantic novel, *La Virgen de Borriquen* (The Puerto Rican Virgin). Then there was José de Diego a poet and political writer advocating Puerto Rico's independence, who wrote *A Puerto Rico (To Puerto Rico);*

José Gautier Benitez' *Canto a Puerto Rico (Hymn to Puerto Rico);* Santiago Vidarte's *Cancionero de Puerto Rico (Songster of Puerto Rico).* Eugenio Maria de Hostos y Bonilla, was a writer and teacher—his works fill twenty volumes. Expressing some aspects of Puerto Rican literature, he wrote, "More painful than bullets, more painful than ailments are the sufferings of the fatherland," and "By a will of nature, it is the woman who shapes the heart."

There was Francisco Gonzalo Marin, another exile poet who expressed his deep sentiments for Puerto Rican independence. There were historians such as Salvador Brau, who wrote of the poverty of the peasants and the social ills of his country.

Lola Rodríquez de Tió a poetess, wrote the verses for the national anthem *La Borinquena,* that was sung at "Grito de Lares" during the uprising in 1868. Both Muñoz Marin and his father, Muñoz Rivera, were poets and politicians. In later years, too, were René Marques' *Ensayos (Essays)* and Antonio Pedreira's *Insulismo.* In literature should be mentioned the writers: Pedro Juan Soto Enrique Laguerre, Manuel Meridez Ballister, Coucha Melendez; and the poets, Clara Lair, Evanistto Rivera Chevremona, Luis Hernandez Aquiro, Numia Vicens, Julia de Burgos, and Luis Pales Matos. The verses of the last two have been set to music by singer-composer Alberto Carrion and by the very popular Lucecita Benitez. Concerts have been given by them in the University of Puerto Rico Theatre backed by a thirty-five member orchestra conducted by Pedro Rivera Toledo and a six-member chorus that included Wilson Torres, Nelly Croatto, and Glen Monroig, all popular singers in their own rights. Among ballad-makers, too, is Rafael Hernandez.

All Puerto Ricans love music and dance. One despotic Spanish governor is said to have remarked that the Puerto Rican people can be governed with a whip and a violin.

Local music is mostly Spanish melodies with an African rhythm and almost all are meant for dancing. There is the plena (which resembles the West Indian calypso) and the danza (dance). The Puerto Rican national anthem is based on the music of the danza. There is an underlying note of nostalgia and sadness in the danza. Musician Juan Monel Campos, born in 1855, was one of the best known composers of the danza.

The salsa of today is more Spanish than African, but there is also a mixing of salsa and jazz. The "baile de bomba" usually danced in special locations on the island, particularly in Loiza Aldea, strongly reflects its African origin. In the rural areas, the traditional songs, called "décimas" since they are verses of ten lines, are accompanied by a form of guitar, which has four strings and is called the "cuatro" and

At Puerto Rico's LeLoLai Festival, Jibaro dancers follow a traditional Jibaro banquet. The Jibaros, or mountain farmers, have been major contibutors to Puerto Rico's music and dance traditions. Local music is mostly for dancing. The original 'jibaros' clothes were similar in style, but were not nearly as fancy as those shown in this picture. Shoes were seldom worn, since only the rich could afford them. (PHOTO COURTESY OF PUERTO RICO TOURISM DEVELOPMENT.)

is essentially of Spanish derivation. The old percussion instruments of the Indians, however, are still used. Gourds with seeds, and the drums of both Indian and African origin continue to have an important place in the music of Puerto Rico. The Indians used a conch shell for a trumpet sound.

Recently, folkloric groups have been formed. They dance the old traditional dances and wear the old traditional costumes.

Traditionally there were two types of dances: those of high society influenced by the dances of European courts and society, such as the minuet, the cotillon, the waltz, and the mazurka. The second type was called "bailes," the popular dances. Some of these were folk dances for groups, as exist in all peasant societies. Some were similar to square dances but with a different type of music and a different beat. Many were danced barefoot, since the people then did not have the luxury of shoes. The "bomba" was a special African-Puerto Rican dance. There have been dances such as the "upa" borrowed from Cuba, and the tango and flamenco popular in Spain and Latin America.

San Juan also has an excellent Corps de Ballet, and throughout the island there are schools of ballet, and competitions held once a year between the groups.

Besides those who play dance music, there are also, of course, Puerto Rican musicians who play the classical and modern music of Europe and the United States. The Figueroa family all have great talent. There is also Jesus Sanroma, educated at the New England Conservatory of Music, and a soloist for a long time of the Boston Symphony Orchestra. Interestingly, since he was playing there at the time Koussevitzky was conductor, he learned to speak Russian. He is an outstanding pianist specializing in playing Rachmaninoff's works. Among other musicians are Olga Iglesias, Maria Esther Robles and, Jack Delano. The latter wrote and composed thirteen-hour long programs on the symphonies of Beethoven, Brahms, and Berlioz for the Public Broadcasting System television.

The Casals Festivals of San Juan are known worldwide. Though Casals himself was born in Spain, his mother was a Puerto Rican. She herself was musical and married a teacher of music. Casals made his home in San Juan. Under his direction, Puerto Rico formed a fine symphony orchestra.

The first symphony concert given in Puerto Rico was in 1803. During the last quarter of the last century, scholarships were given for students to go to Europe and the States to study music. At the same time an academy of music was set up in San Juan. Today the San Juan Conservatory of Music is open to any talented youngster without fee but he has to be dedicated, ready to undergo long hours of practice. If he fails, there is a long list of others waiting to take his place. The Puerto Rican Symphony Orchestra, as well as giving free concerts in San Juan, also travels throughout the island to give concerts for people who live in towns where they would rarely have an opportunity of hearing good music.

San Juan also has an excellent opera company, with some singers of exceptional voice.

There are several popular Puerto Rican singers, such as Danny Rivera and Lucecita Benitez whose records are sold throughout the Caribbean, South America, and the United States.

For drama, there is the Tapia Theater built in 1830, named after Puerto Rico's first prominent playwright, Alejandro Tapia y Rivera. He wrote romantic plays about the idyllic love affair between Capitan Don Cristobal de Sotomayer and Princess Guanina, sister of the supreme chief, Guaybana; and about the daring pirate, Cofresi.

The Tapia Theater has been restored recently. It is a small gem of a theater with a charming horseshoe-shaped interior. The seats have been imported from Spain. Here, plays given by talented Puerto

For those interested in the dramatic arts, there is the Tapia Theatre built in 1832 and named after Alejandro Tapia y Rivera, one of Puerto Rico's earliest playwrights. (PHOTO COURTESY OF INSTITUTO DE CULTURA PUERTORRIQUEÑA.)

Rican actors, range from classical to ultramodern. The huge auditorium at the University of Puerto Rico is also used for plays, concerts, opera, and ballet. There are also several small dramatic groups who perform mostly modern plays by aspiring Puerto Rican dramatists. An annual festival of drama has become a major yearly event.

In painting, the first well-known Puerto Rican artist is José Campeche. His themes were religious, but he also painted the social personages of his time, including the governors. A later nineteenth century painter was Francis Oller. One of his paintings, *El Estudiante (The Student)* hangs in the Louvre in Paris. At one time, he was a painter at the Court of Charles III of Spain.

Today, there are numerous exhibitions of paintings, sculpture and crafts in the art shops in Old San Juan, in the restored Dominican Convent near El Morro, in the gallery of the University of Puerto Rico. Among well-known Puerto Rican painters and artists today are Julio Roasado del Valle, Francisco Rodo, Epifario Irrizarry Rafael Infino, Lorenzo Homar, Luis Hernandedez Cruz, and Angel Botello.

There are numerous exhibitions of paintings, sculpture, and crafts. Three visitors to Puerto Rico examine a ceramics exhibit in the Dominican convent. This huge, beautiful building was started by the Dominican friars in 1523, two years after the founding of San Juan. The Dominican Fathers left it when all Puerto Rican monasteries were closed in 1838. (PHOTO COURTESY OF PUERTO RICO TOURISM DEVELOPMENT.)

Much of it is abstract and modern. Much has been influenced by Mexican painters, beginning with Rivera, who became a muralist. In Puerto Rico, the art of painting murals has flourished in recent years. They are to be found in banks, universities, and on the walls of the "caserios," the low-cost housing developments. A great number of the murals have old Indian themes, painted in bright, primitive colors.

Though Puerto Ricans are proud of their own culture and heritage, there is a small group that proudly proclaims a pride in their Spanish lineage. Their members can be compared to those of the Daughters of the American Revolution in the States. They own a fine building near the Capital called Casa de España (House of Spain). Here all upper-class girls make their debuts, and on one night a year one of them is crowned queen. Thousands of dollars are spent on exquisite ball gowns for this special event.

One of San Juan's many art galleries featuring contemporary Puerto Rican art and sculpture. (PHOTO COURTESY OF PUERTO RICO TOURISM DEVELOPMENT.)

Exterior of Ponce's Museo de Arte in Puerto Rico. Designed by Edward Durell Stone, the museum has won the American Institute of Architect's Honor Award. It contains a balanced exhibition of five centuries of European and American paintings and sculptures—including works by Velazquez, Gainsborough, and Van Dyke. (PHOTO COURTESY OF PUERTO RICO INFORMATION SERVICE.)

The dramatic central staircases of the Ponce Art Museum located on Puerto Rico's south coast: the home of one of the finest art collections in the Caribbean. (PHOTO COURTESY OF PUERTO RICO TOURISM DEVELOPMENT.)

There has been a revival recently in the crafts as well as in the arts. The making of hammocks has survived since the time of the early Indians. They are of different sizes and colors. There is the "Matrimonio" hammock, for the married couple; a hammock wide enough to wrap around oneself on chilly evenings; a hammock that takes the place of a crib for a baby in the Puerto Rican hills, called by the old Indian name, "coy." People take hammocks to the beach when they go on picnics and hang them between the palms so that the head of the family, or the laziest member of the group, can get his siesta. Fruit vendors on side streets will settle their stalls in the shade of two trees, where a hammock can be hung and a relaxing rest taken between sales periods.

Very fine embroidery and lace work used to be made at home by women and children. Mayaguez was particularly well-known for this industry. Since the mothers and daughters doing this work gained only a few centavos (pennies) for long hours of eye-straining work, the art is dying. Women now put their delicate skills into much better paying jobs in clothing or pharmaceutical factories.

Decorative ironwork has long been a talent of Spanish and Puerto Rican craftsmen. The filagreed balcony railing, the ornate moulding and louvered doors make attractive one of the many restored homes in Old San Juan. (PHOTO COURTESY OF PUERTO RICO TOURISM DEVELOPMENT.)

Pottery-making has been an art in Puerto Rico since its very earliest times. Pottery-making has had periods of flourishing and periods of neglect. Today it is experiencing a revival of interest. Pottery of all types are being made from pots and vases to figurines. These are often derived from old Indian designs.

Woven mats and rugs can be found in Old San Juan shops, in the hills, and in such places as Cidra. Here an artisan will make special patterns to required shapes and sizes.

Ironwork on houses is decorative work with dozens of different

The Calle Cristo Chapel, one of the architectural treasures in Old San Juan. According to legend the chapel was built by grateful parents in the 18th century, when their son survived a potentially fatal riding accident on this spot. (PHOTO COURTESY OF PUERTO RICO TOURISM DEVELOPMENT.)

designs and patterns. Besides being decorative, it also keeps out burglars. Elaborate modern sculpture is also being fashioned in iron. One well-known sculptor in the medium is Rafael Ferrer, the brother of actor Jose Ferrer. There is also the modern statue of *La Rogativa,* commemorating the religious procession in 1795, which according to legend drove British attackers away when San Juan was being occupied by them. Among the modern sculptors are Lindsay Doen, Luisa Geigel, John Balossi, Tomas Batista, and Francisco Vazquez Diaz, known in sculpture as Compostela. That interest is wide in modern art is evinced by the long well-illustrated articles each week in the newspapers, describing the local showings, written by university art professor Felix Bonilla Norat.

The artistry of the Indians in works of gold had been carried on by the artisans who arrived from Spain. Their first works in cathedrals and churches began to appear as long ago as 1529 and were reflections of the skills in Europe at that time. The copies of what were at first Spanish art were developed into individual styles by Puerto Ricans. Their art grew directly from their own creativeness within the milieu of the island and from influences from Latin America. Mexico in particular was a strong influence. The work of Puerto Rican artisans in their turn spread throughout the Spanish-speaking world,

Much of the artistic work through the centuries has been connected with the churches. This carved and painted cross is one of the many pieces of antique religious art gathered in the Porta Coeli museum. (PHOTO COURTESY OF PUERTO RICO TOURISM DEVELOPMENT.)

so that their work can be seen in Mexico and Spain, as well as on the island.

Much of the artistic work through the centuries has been connected with the churches: the architecture itself and its embellishments: the paintings, the altar work, the chalices, and all other appurtenances of the Catholic ceremonies.

Much wealth was acquired by the Church: golden altars, golden candlesticks, and figures of the Virgin and Child. To a great extent, gold was concentrated in the embellishment of the churches. But recently on display in San Juan were, among nonreligious objects, a golden sword and a golden filigree crown.

The period of the greatest flowering of Puerto Rican goldsmith and silversmith art was during the period of the eighteenth and early nineteenth century. This is considered the Golden Age of their work which was exquisite, beautiful, and intricately crafted. In the nineteenth century, when cheap plating processes were taking the place of the precious metals, the art was debased and the number of those carrying on the centuries-old skill dropped. Yet, at the time of the American takeover in 1898, there were still nearly 200 registered goldsmiths and silversmiths on the island.

The style of the Puerto Rican artists is European derived from the baroque, roccoco, neo-classic, and romantic periods. But there is always the individual personal touch of the Puerto Rican craftsman. This work differs from the simple, primitive art of the "santeros." It is an elaborate, artistic expression of the natural beauty of the island. Ornate golden chalices, flying silver angels, a sleeping Christ child in silver and wood are some of the treasures to be found in the island's cathedrals and churches.

Oddly, the sun worshiped by the Tainos as a life-giving god, continued to be represented throughout the centuries in the confines of the Catholic Church. There are numbers of golden sunbursts to be seen in the work of mestizo artisans. The moon which also had its place in Taino religion is found among later silversmith's artistry. *La Torrecilla*, made toward the end of the sixteenth century and used in processions in San Juan Cathedral, is topped by outstretched pelican wings. This is surely the special feature of an early artisan of the island, who had looked out at the ocean and seen such a sight as he was perfecting his design.

The Catholic Church was for centuries the center of life for the people. The churches were places of beauty, where rest and peace could be found. The pomp and ceremony were colorful adjuncts of life, to which the people gladly gave their "centavos" and "pesetas" to help its further adornment.

Puerto Rico's official seal illustrates Saint John the Baptist, since originally San Juan was the name given to the island in 1511. The motto reads, "Joannes est nomen ejus," meaning "John is his name." The seal shows a lamb, a white flag with a superimposed cross, and the initials "F" and "I." These intertwined initials are for King Ferdinand and Queen Isabella. The border of the seal shows two castles, two red lions, two crosses and two banners. The castles represent Isabella, queen of Castile; and the lions, Ferdinand, King of the province of Leon. (Aragon) Their marriage consolidated a large part of Spain. This was the royal couple who financed Columbus' discovery of the New World.

An old statue entitled "The Immaculate Conception," which stands in the 17th century chapel of Porta Coeli in San German. (PHOTO COURTESY OF INSTITUTO DE CULTURA PUERTORRIQUEÑA.)

An example of the restoration of houses in Old San Juan. In 1949, Old San Juan was declared an Historic Zone where all construction is regulated. Characteristics are balconies, wide entrance halls and interior patios. Note the differences between the old and the restored houses. (PHOTO COURTESY OF PUERTO RICO INFORMATION SERVICE.)

The Instituto de Cultura Puertorriqueño, whose seal is a Spaniard flanked on one side by an Indian and on the other by a black, celebrated its twentieth anniversary in 1978. It is now housed in the beautiful restored Dominican Convent. There are seventy other cultural centers and fourteen museums on the island. Since they are mostly in Old San Juan, schoolchildren are brought in buses to visit them. These cultural centers and museums also hold interest for visitors to the island who are anxious to know more of Puerto Rico than what its big hotels and wonderful beaches tell.

Among these cultural centers is the Dominican Convent in Old San Juan which goes back to the sixteenth century. It is a magnificent structure, with its high arches opening on to the inner courtyard and

At the top of the hill on Calle Cristo in Old San Juan, a restored wooden balcony overlooks the streets. Baskets of sprengeri fern and peperomia–called paz del hogar *(peace of the home)—hand over the railing.* (PHOTO COURTESY OF PUERTO RICO TOURISM DEVELOPMENT.)

its balconies railed with old wooden Spanish ballisters. There is also the museum of the Puerto Rican family showing the rooms and furniture of a middle class household in the years of Spanish domination. La Casa Blanca, built in 1529 for Ponce de Leon's family, is the new home of this museum, which includes furnishings, paintings and art objects of the sixteenth and seventeenth centuries. Then there is the Caso del Libro (House of the Book) installed in a charming eighteenth century house. Here early books and manuscripts are displayed. There is the Museum of Military History in Fort San Jeronimo. Field Marshall Alejandro O'Reilly was responsible for its reinforcements during his stay. In architecture, even though there

A well-restored street in Old San Juan. (PHOTO BY FRANK H. WADSWORTH.)

is much that is almost ultra-modern today, in many houses and buildings the old Spanish style is still reflected.

Also on the island is the Museum and Archeological Park in Utuado, where the old Indian ballpark was discovered. There is a museum of Religious Art in Porta Coeli in San German, the town where Ponce de Leon made his first headquarters. In the hotel section of modern San Juan is El Centro, where one can find displays of artifacts as well as arts and crafts and where a folkloric group in costume dances the old dances to the old music.

The wooden santos made by the 'jibaros', could be bought a few decades ago for as little as three dollars each. Now they are possessions of considerable value and some have been given to American presidents on state occasions.

A painting by Campeche could be bought at one time for one hundred dollars. Now it is difficult to obtain one at any price since there are so many collectors wanting his work. The best modern

The fine administration building of the U. S. Department of Agriculture is designed in Spanish style. (PHOTO COURTESY OF U. S. DEPARTMENT OF AGRICULTURE.)

Wooden and colored santos *representing the Three Kings, with Melchior, the black King, in the middle riding a white horse.* (PHOTO COURTESY OF INSTITUTO DE CULTURA PUERTORRIQUEÑA.)

A santo's *group showing the flight from Egypt, executed in wood and painted in bright colors.* (PHOTO COURTESY OF INSTITUTO DE CULTURA PUERTORRIQUEÑA.)

Puerto Rican painters today can obtain several thousand dollars for each of their works.

Most of this revival in Puerto Rican history and culture is very recent and started with the opening of the Instituto and its first director, Ricardo Alegria. Today, Puerto Ricans have a sense of their past.

Writing verse is popular with Puerto Ricans. At the beginning of the twentieth century, it was the fashion of the men to take postcards, write their own compositions on the backs, and send them to their sweethearts. The women kept a collection of the cards from their various swains.

There are also makers of masks, mostly simple masks carved from coconuts and painted in many vivid colors resulting in an outlandish effect. Some masks have painted black faces and wild expressions. They may even have a ring inserted through the nose. They all express a certain vitality of feeling.

Skills which go back to both Indian and African roots are appearing in a renaissance of old crafts such as wood carving. This is particularly true of the "santos." The tradition for their making goes back to the time of the Spanish Conquest. Spain could not supply the number of

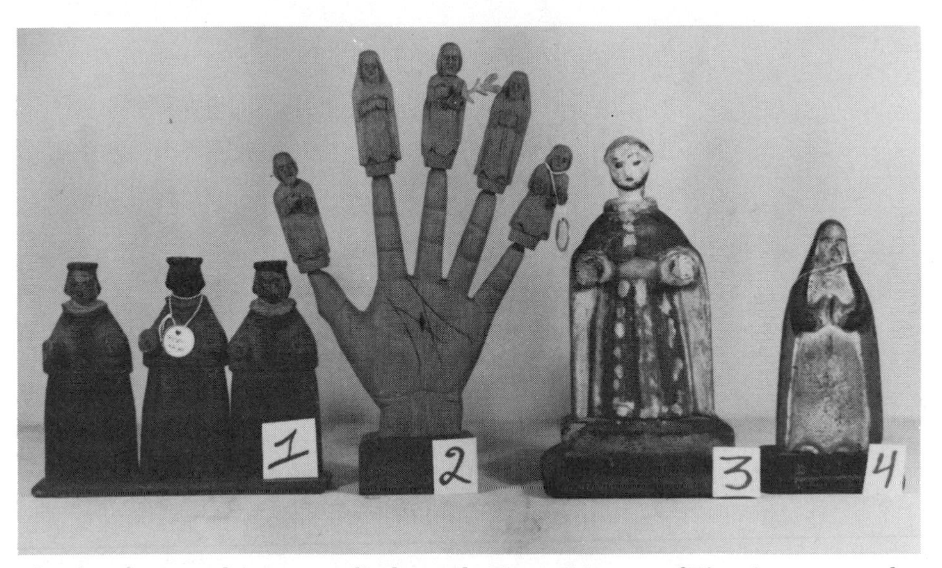

A series of santos *that were on display at the Boston Museum of Fine Arts among other museums in the States. The hand with the stigmata and figures on each finger is particularly interesting.* (PHOTO COURTESY OF INSTITUTO DE CULTURA PUERTORRIQUEÑA.)

religious images required in the colonies. The people, used to the "cemies," the household gods in their homes, were eager when these had to be replaced, to have the carven images of the new religion. They began to carve their own from the examples they saw in the churches: the Virgin Mary, Christ, saints, angels, and apostles. Gradually, there grew up in the villages, "santeros," the makers of "santos," using the old Indian skills of carving in wood or chiseling stone. As the art developed, the "santeros" were not content to be merely copyists, but creatively developed images of their own. Sometimes their work was of a single figure; sometimes of a group; sometimes more ambitiously they set out to carve from wood, scenes from the Bible stories they had learned. They would depict the Three Kings (always a great favorite) including the black Melchior on a white horse. There were carvings of The Flight into Egypt, of Christ as a child with Saint Joseph, and of Mary. When they had carved the figures, they would color them. Saint Francis, for instance, appeared in a brown robe such as that worn by the Franciscan monks. Almost all the colors were bright and several colors were used on each santo. Today the old santos are of considerable value, and many of the best of them have been collected and can be seen in the museums in Old San Juan and in the University of Puerto Rico.

There is no cultural poverty in Puerto Rico.

5
The End of the Spanish Era

PUERTO Rico did not take part in the great movement in the early nineteenth century in which all the countries of Latin America broke from the motherland. Bolivar had intended that the Spanish Antilles—that is the islands of Cuba, Puerto Rico, and Santo Domingo should be included in his confederation. But Cuba and Puerto Rico remained loyal to the Crown. In fact, in some instances, Puerto Rican troops were sent to South America to help put down rebellions, and some loyalists to Spain fled South America to find refuge on the island.

However, some liberalized policies were begun in 1815. These policies gave more independence of action to the island in conducting its own affairs. Spain was afraid that if this were not done, severe discontent might erupt in the colony. Therefore, Bolivar's and San Martin's successes on the mainland caused some indirect benefit to Puerto Rico.

One of these liberalized policies was allowing the mayors of the towns, that is civilians, to dispense local justice. This had always been handled by the military. Of greater significance was the law abolishing the slave trade in 1817, though it took three years to implement it, and even then was largely disregarded by most plantation owners. Slavery did not end until decreed in 1873 by the National Assembly of the Spanish Republic.

A palm avenue leads to a sugar planter's hacienda (estate house). The black woman carries a large basket on her head as well as a load in her arms. While slavery was abolished in 1875, it was largely disregarded by the plantation owners.

With a revolutionary movement in Spain in which the King was overthrown, the 1812 Constitution governing Puerto Rico was restored. It had been previously suspended. This led in 1820 to the forming of the first embryo political party by a group of islanders under the title of Sociedad de Liberales Amantes de la Patria (Society of Liberal Lovers of the Country). In the following year, when the neighboring island of the Dominican Republic proclaimed its independence, a group arose calling for Puerto Rico to do the same. This was the first independence group. To placate these groups further, the Republican government of Spain appointed the first civilian governor to the island. But with the restoration of the monarchy, in

Spain both reformist and independence groups were suppressed. A period of reaction ensued.

Most of the appointed Spanish governors were despots. Their purpose was to see that "law and order" were maintained and any disturbing elements were crushed.

The military garrison stamped its character as strongly as ever on the island. The Church continued to play a reactionary part.

Military jurisdiction and a strong military presence gave Puerto Rico its conservative character. The Church reinforced the authority of the military. The Spaniards said they had come to the New World "to save souls" as well as to find gold. We have already stated that Dominican friars came with the first ships and later Franciscan monks arrived. The Holy Inquisition set up its power first in Puerto Rico in the sixteenth century, and it continued until 1813 when it was abolished. During a period of reaction in Spain a decade later, it was again restored and operated as late as 1823 to 1834. The victims, burned at the stake or broken at the wheel before a watching crowd, were usually poor blacks. Their crime was that they had mixed remembered African spiritism with Catholic dogma.

Monasteries had been closed a few years earlier, and for a while the monks and friars were homeless. With the restoration of the Inquisition, the buildings were given back to their owners, only to be closed

The Military jurisdiction and a strong military presence gave Puerto Rico its conservative character. (PHOTO SHOWS SPANISH OFFICERS STATIONED IN PUERTO RICO BEFORE THE AMERICAN OCCUPATION.)

again in 1835. All churches, however, remained open. These interesting and often beautiful churches have been well-preserved providing historical witness to the island's Spanish, Catholic past. The earliest convent for women in Puerto Rico was established in 1651. An aristocratic Spanish woman opened her house for this purpose to six of her women relatives, but she had to make a handsome payment to the King for this privilege. He was eager for any possible source of revenue.

There was no other religion than Roman Catholic on the island.

The Bishopric of Puerto Rico was the largest in the world since it covered the other Spanish islands in the Caribbean and parts of South America. There were no other churches until the first Anglican church was built in Poncé in 1873. It was built in sections sent out from England. It was the only such church in all of Spain's colonies, and remained the only Protestant Church on the island until after the American occupation.

So hand in hand the military and the Catholic Church ruled Spain's island subjects. However, fifty years later than Spain's other colonies in the New World, rebellion against confining rules and regulations was developing in Puerto Rico and Cuba.

In 1868 an outbreak against Spanish rules occurred. This is known in Puerto Rico as El Grito de Lares because it began in the little mountain town of Lares.

In 1868, in neighboring Santo Domingo, a Puerto Rican committee was formed calling for full Puerto Rican independence from Spain. This was under the leadership of Dr. Ramon Emeterio Betances. Through emissaries, small supporting groups were organized all over the island. A shipload of arms was made ready to help in a projected uprising but the authorities learned of the planned revolt and seized the ship en route in St. Thomas. The rebels had to go forward without this decisive help from outside. They moved into the town of Lares, where they set up a Provisional Government. Here the revolutionists who started the three-day outbreak, proclaimed the Republic, flew a specially designed flag, and had a *Te Deum* sung in the local church, sanctifying their cause. From all over the island many hurried to answer the call of "freedom or death." San Sebastian was seized, then Camuy, Moca and Quebradillas; all towns on the western end of the island. A national anthem had been composed by Felix Astol called *La Borinqueña,* with lyrics written by the poetess Lola Rodriquez de Tio. *La Borinqueña* is still Puerto Rico's national anthem, though the lyrics have been changed.

In the second half of the nineteenth century, those merely calling for more reforms and measures of self-government were put in prison in El Morro castle. This led to some seeing revolution as the only solution. Later, the first real Puerto Rican political party was formed. The Spanish Crown and the Spanish governors of the island had not until that time felt it necessary to allow Puerto Ricans that privilege. The short revolution, El Grito de Lares, though unsuccessful, had caused this concession. The party was named Partido Liberal Reformista (Liberal Reform Party). It demanded more liberal reforms and more measures of self-government. A leader of the reformist movement was Baldorioty de Castro (the wide highway from the airport to San Juan bears his name). He was elected as a representative to the Spanish Cortes (Parliament) but he could obtain none of the political reforms requested. It was then that he created the Autonomist Party, Partido Autonomista Puertorriqueño, and for this was put in jail. Another nineteenth-century reformist leader was the talented romantic writer and poet, José Gautier Benitez. He called for more self-government for Puerto Rico, but did not wish to break the ties with Spain, where he had been educated. Among those who wished to be fully assimilated into the Spanish empire was José Julian Acosta. He, too, had studied in Spain, like most of his educated compatriots. Being more conservative than Baldoriorty de Castro, he did not join the autonomista party. Even so, he was imprisoned for his calls for reform and for the abolition of slavery. He helped establish the Ateneo Puertorriqueño, an institution for the furtherance of Puerto Rican culture and history.

An opposing party was formed under the leadership of Segundo Ruiz Belvis, who had been an Autonomista, and Dr. Ramon Betances, a practicing physician who is honored today as one of Puerto Rico's patriots. He called for full independence, and wanted to establish Bolivar's idea of a confederation of the three Spanish islands of Puerto Rico, the Dominican Republic, and Cuba. He was exiled from the island and lived first in New York and then in France.

The next "independentista" of prominence was Puerto Rican patriot Eugenio María de Hostos. (There is a holiday each year in his honor on the island.) Also forced into exile for his views, he joined Cuban revolutionaries in New York, hoping with them to obtain the independence of Spain's last two colonies in the Western Hemisphere. He made an attempt to see President William McKinley to urge him not to let American troops occupy either Cuba or Puerto Rico. When the United States did take over in 1898, he still urged independence.

Another poet and patriot, who joined his brother revolutionaries in exile in New York, was Pachin Marin. After his newspaper in Puerto Rico was banned, he published it in New York. Later he died in Cuba,

A squad of the Fifth U. S. Cavalry rides through a Puerto Rican village in 1898 during the American invasion. Puerto Rican patriot Eugenie Maria de Hostos urged President William McKinley not to let American troops occupy the island.

helping the fight for independence there. Still another writer and poet, José de Diego (whom Puerto Ricans also honor with a holiday) was to join the New York exiles. He had propounded his views at first in the island Legislature, and he also supported the idea of an Antillean Confederation of an independent Puerto Rico, Dominican Republic, and Cuba.

However, pointing up the cleavage of political views, on the island Roberto H. Todd and Dr. Julio Henna, two other exiles in New York, met with President McKinley requesting that Puerto Rico should be included in the invasion plans for Cuba. They offered to lead United States forces into the island.

By the end of the nineteenth century, however, the autonomistas had been victorious in having gained those aspects of self-government which they had demanded. Spain's power and grandeur, which had been at its height in the century following the Conquest, were now at their lowest ebb. It was her weakness at this point that led to her making her final concessions. After decades of struggle, Puerto Rico was given a Charter of Autonomy.

Sixteen Congressmen and three Senators were elected with voting rights in the Spanish Cortés. *La Carta Autonomista* could be changed or abolished by mutual consent between Spain and Puerto Rico. Home rule was granted. Puerto Rico was given a voice in the shaping of foreign policy as it affected the island, in decisions in regard to tariff laws, and was given universal male suffrage. The decree was signed in 1897, and after elections, the first Puerto Rican government was enthusiastically established in February of 1898 with Luis Muñoz Rivera as governor. It was the closest that Puerto Rico ever came to independence. The new government had been in office only a few months when the United States invaded the island and the political gains were obliterated.

A young officer in the Spanish Army stationed at El Morro in 1898, recalled how, his regiment had reacted to the American conquest. He remembered how he had stood with tears streaming down his face, saluting, for the last time, the Spanish flag. It had waved in the breeze so proudly for so many centuries on that small headland thrust into the Atlantic Ocean between two great continents. Its lowering signified the end of Spanish possessions in the Western Hemisphere. For him and his countrymen, it was the end of an era, and for many like him, a loss like the loss of a mother.

Under the Treaty of Paris in December, 1898, Spain granted the United States possession of Puerto Rico and the Philippines, and with the Platt Amendment, a few years later, the right to interfere in Cuban affairs. By way of compensation, Spain was given twenty million dollars.

Two very large volumes of almost eight hundred pages in a 12″ × 16″ trim size entitled *Our Islands* describe and give statistics of the islands that the United States took over in 1898. The book was commissioned by the U.S. Army and has an introduction by Major General Joseph Wheeler. Narrative and descriptions are by José de Olivares. In the account of Puerto Rico at that time, much of its material supports the work of other authors. However, much of it shows how strange the newcomers found Puerto Rico and the inhabitants. There is a tendency in the volumes to make the Spaniards, the "bad guys," and the Americans, "the good guys." Advice is given concerning the best investments to make in the island. The book suggests how the Puerto Ricans should be treated by Americans. It reiterates the view of others as to the lushness of the island and with what abundance all the many fruits grow, the attractiveness of the women; the politeness of the people; and the hardworking character of the laboring man. It gives an insight both of the viewed and the viewers in their first meeting.

From the beginning, it was decided to change the name from Puerto Rico to Porto Rico. As the book comments, "There are few historical instances wherein the language of the vanquished nation

A tobacco field up in the mountains is shaded by nets against the hot sun. Tobacco comprised part of the exports of Puerto Rico in 1898. (PHOTO COURTESY OF THE DEPARTMENT OF AGRICULTURE.)

Tobacco being grown alongside tobacco drying sheds in the mountains. (PHOTO COURTESY OF DEPARTMENT OF AGRICULTURE.)

Cattle, first brought over by the Spaniards in the 16th century, formed part of the island's trade in 1898. These are a fairly recent cross-breed from Brahmin bulls. (PHOTO COURTESY OF THE U. S. DEPARTMENT OF AGRICULTURE.)

Outside a hat store in the 1890s. The owner stands beside the hats and the straws that went into their making. At the side are the employees, neatly dressed but bare-footed.

was adopted by the conqueror. 'Puerto Rico' is un-American, as well as harsh and affected, when the effort is made to pronounce it by anyone unfamiliar with the Spanish tongue. Moreover, we prefer all things American, without the least taint or coloring of Spanish."

The book proceeds to say that the people are found as by all previous visitors (and as the Conquistadores found the Tainos) gentle and hospitable.

The land is beautiful and productive, with the mountains rounded and able to be cultivated almost to the top. The soil is fertile and produces abundant crops with little cultivation. The scenery all over the island is most picturesque.

Girls sorting coffee at Yauco. In the book Our Islands *the reporter in 1898 wrote that all the girls were bare-footed and dressed usually in a single garment. Some of them were quite beautiful, he said, and all had "bright, intelligent faces."*

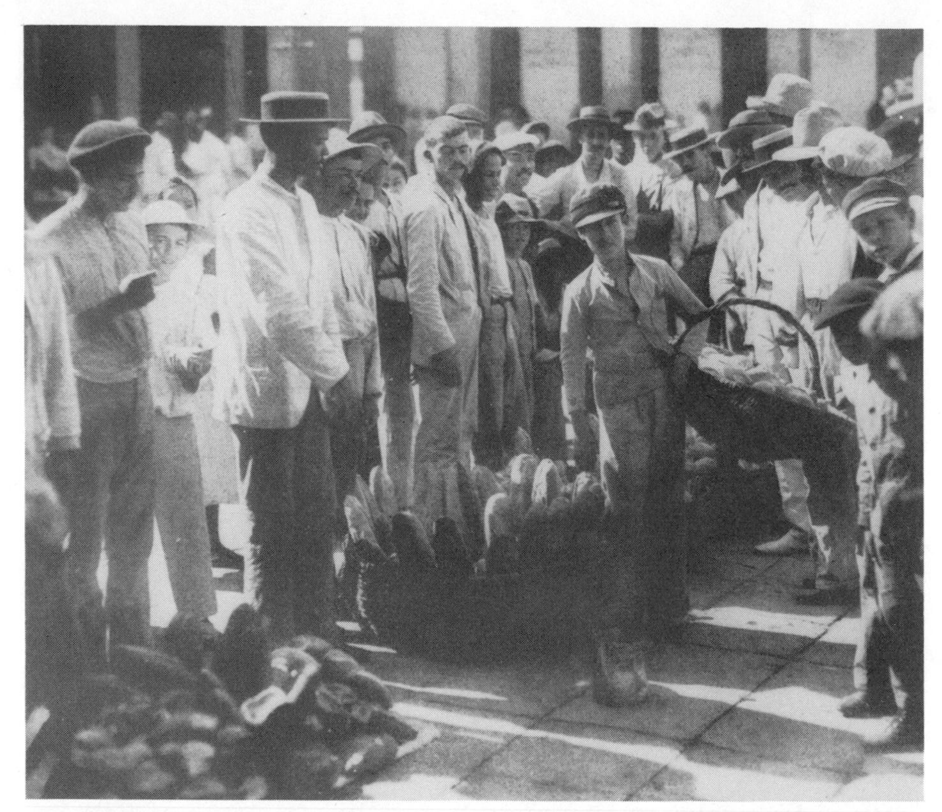

The bread market in San Juan in 1898. Puerto Rico still makes the delicious long loaves of pan de agua *(water bread).*

"They are willing to work," says the writer of Our Islands. *A group of cigarette factory employees standing in the street outside their cabins. At the end of the nineteenth century the factory employed over 500 workers.*

The commerce is given for 1896, as the best in the island's history. It amounted to over $36 million dollars with the imports and exports each about eighteen million. Exports were: sugar, coffee, molasses, tobacco, fruits, nuts, spices, perfume, cosmetics, chemicals, drugs, dyes, timber, salt, and beef cattle. Imports included rice, flour, dairy products, iron, steel, and general manufactured articles.

However, says the writer, "Our tariff regulations are working a serious injury to the industries of the island." The trade with Spain had almost disappeared, "while at the same time our tariff practically closes the door of American markets to all Porto Rican products. The result is that industries of all kinds are languishing, produce rots in the hands of the planters or the merchants, a large percentage of the people are idle, while want and suffering stalk hand in hand over the island."

In the book, it is suggested that the people, who welcomed "the flag of stars with such joy," should not be treated so badly or they would "regret their union with the great Republic." Profound statesmanship was needed.

The newcomers were shocked by the nudity of the children of the poor. These children did not wear any clothes for the first few years of their lives.

The civil administration was in local hands "of boards of health, charities, education, public works, etc. In all of which the natives have representation. The customs are collected by army officers, assisted by natives, and the rule is everywhere to give the natives the preference in all kinds of employment. They are willing to work and eager to learn."

In *Our Islands* we are told that Americans found that crime was low. Though a bit of rum seemed part of a Puerto Rican laborer's diet, there was little sign of drunkenness.

Americans were surprised at the seeming complete lack of color discrimination, especially those who came from the southern states.

"Among the higher classes, the people are refined and cultivated. They are honorable, honest, and in the Spanish way, God-fearing. Their home feeling is especially strong and family ties seem to be regarded with a sacredness unknown among the colder-blooded races."

In regard to the teaching of English, elementary readers had already been ordered by 1900. Maps on the schoolroom walls were of the United States. There were also charts of the chief events in American history and of American heroes. Patriotic song books about the States were introduced.

During this time sewing women worked from 7 a.m. to 6 p.m. for fifteen cents a day including their breakfast and dinner. A fine dress was made for $2.40 and a lady's linen night dress, including the material, tucked at the yoke and trimmed with lace and insertion, with buttons as desired, cost only forty-five cents. Maids received three to four dollars a month. First class cooks, who also did the marketing, received six dollars a month. They were all "clean and nice looking."

Material for construction of all kinds, cement, building stone, lime, and sand, were used "with great skill" by the men. The people were poor but seemed happy.

While poor, there was no actual destitution until after the great hurricane of 1899, one year after the American occupation.

Wealthy families on the other hand, reared their children, and especially their daughters in idle luxury, waited on hand and foot by servants. Learning the graceful accomplishments of embroidery, music, and painting, they were also given some measure of education by lay brothers. And at all times, the duenña was at hand.

An American writer who attended an aristocratic ball in San Juan describes the beautiful, modest, but helpless Puerto Rican girls.

> "I venture you have never seen a prettier sight. They are straight and slender and everyone a brunette. What beautiful hair they have, black as the patent leatheı shoes of the men. What pretty eyes they have! They are large, black, and liquid, with long lashes and rather

A flamenco dancer poses regally. She is typical of the beautiful Puerto Rican girls, having dark hair and honey-colored faces. (PHOTO COURTESY OF PUERTO RICAN TOURISM DEVELOPMENT.)

> heavy brows, which are accentuated by their pale brunette faces. Their faces are sweet, full of fun, but refined. They keep up the dance throughout the evening. It is only while dancing that they have the chance of being alone with their beaux, for according to Spanish custom, when they sit down, they must take their places by their married sisters, mothers, or aunts, who act as duennas. Every girl had a fan which she kept always in motion. She fans herself three times and then with a twist of the wrist throws the fold of the fan together. Another twist and it is open in the opposite way and she is fanning herself most coquettishly."

In the twentieth century, as in the sixteenth century, a new adjustment had to be made by the inhabitants of the island to a new language, new customs, and new traditions. Religious adjustments, too, had to be made between predominantly white Anglo-Saxon Protestants and Spanish, Catholic mestizos.

6
From Spanish to American Hands

SO the transfer took place, from a Spanish administration three thousand miles away in Europe, to a North American administration. The capital of the United States was 1500 miles away and her original thirteen states had grown since 1775. Now, with the new acquisitions of 1898, she had grown from an area of 350,000 square miles to a territory of over three million square miles.

The United States owns Puerto Rico by "right of conquest," says Senator Henry Jackson.

In the Spanish-American War, the United States fought Spain over Cuba. This was Teddy Roosevelt's "splendid little war." During the last seventeen days of that war, the United States invaded Puerto Rico. Admiral William Sampson and his fleet attacked from the sea but found as the Earl of Cumberland had done, one hundred and fifty years earlier, that a frontal attack by a navy against El Morro was impractical. General Nelson Miles approached by land at Gúanica on the south coast but fought no major battle. It was certainly "a little war," fought for just over two weeks, with a total of fifty American wounded and four dead.

Though the Puerto Ricans and the Spanish garrison soldiers did fight the invading army, there was considerable sympathy for the American take-over. Many Puerto Ricans felt they would enjoy an even more liberal democratic regime than they had recently under the Spaniards.

A Spanish soldier demonstrating his Mauser rifle and his campaign equipment in the period before the U. S. invasion. (PHOTO COURTESY OF INSTITUTO DE CULTURA PUERTORRIQUEÑA.)

The first proclamation to the people by General Miles seemed to foretell this:

> . . . (U.S.) military forces have come to occupy the island of Puerto Rico. . . . This is not a war of devastation but one to give all within the control of its military and naval forces, the advantages and blessings of enlightened civilization. . . .

The military government under the command of General Nelson Miles continued for nearly two years.

In 1901 the "Foraker Act" gave Puerto Rico a civilian governor appointed by the United States President and an Executive Council

A scene in the Plaza at Ponce on July 1st, 1898, some days before the landing of the American forces. The Spanish garrison was receiving the blessing of the Church, and pledging themselves to defend the island against the invaders or die in the effort.

Spanish troops assembled at Guanico in 1898 before they were defeated by the United States Army. (PHOTO COURTESY OF INSTITUTO DE CULTURA PUERTORRIQUEÑA.)

also appointed by the United States President. After the Executive Council was a Chamber of Delegates of thirty-five Puerto Ricans elected by a group of voters limited to those who could read and write and pay taxes. This Chamber could be overridden by the Executive Council and any laws passed could be overridden by the United States Congress. Puerto Ricans had no voice in the Congress of the United States. They had for many decades been allowed to send representatives to the Cortés to plead their causes. In fact, from the beginning of the Conquest, when Fray Bartolomé de Las Casas had pleaded the cause of the Indians before the Spanish courts, there had been means of promoting in Spain, the islanders' point of view.

The island was not made an incorporated territory nor a State of the Union. Its status was left vague as an "unincorporated territory." Neither were the people made citizens of the United States. A new distinction was made in Puerto Rico between "peninsulares"—those from Spain, and the native people. The former could, by a declaration, keep their previous Spanish citizenship. The latter were called "people of Puerto Rico."

Puerto Rico had had its own currency. Now the peso was changed to the dollar, though people today still frequently use the old term. There was devaluation too, and the peasant had to pay more for rice. Devaluation also reduced the coffee revenues of the planters.

There was also a fundamental change in agriculture.

"The Spanish settler was a precursor of the modern entrepreneur. He organized the early economic enterprises through the utilization of cheap labor," writes Professor Arturo Morales-Carrion, former president of the University of Puerto Rico. However, the Spanish did help develop agriculture. In the days of Ponce de Leon, an agricultural experiment station was set up, a royal farm, which was a tropical laboratory, a garden of adaptation for animals and plants.

The Indians had grown corn, sweet potatoes, peppers, tobacco, and cotton. The Conquistadors introduced plantains, bananas, coconuts, mangoes, and citrus fruits. Later they brought in coffee, sugar, and rice. Under Spain, beans, tomatoes, squash, breadfruits, and melons were grown. There was enough of all those products not only for the islanders but for export as well. There were plenty of pigs, goats, chickens, and eggs. At one time, there were the large cattle ranches, later broken up into smaller farms.

Before the invasion of the United States, some 93%, of the arable land was owned and cultivated by Puerto Ricans. There was reasonable diversity of crops. There were many small farmers producing food for their own sustenance and that of the cities. Home produce accounted for about one-third of the total area under

A familiar scene on the road between Ponce and its port, with oxen drawing the carts.

production. Pigs, goats, and cattle dotted about the hills gave the island its rural picture. Within a short while after the American occupation, there was a fundamental change. No longer was there the small landowner raising vegetables which he himself transported either in cart or in a saddle bag to the nearest urban market. The sight of "jibaros" owning pigs, goats, chickens, even a cow, was no longer common.

At the turn of the century Puerto Rico was transformed from the period of family-style haciendas to that of corporate land combines. The smaller haciendas were destroyed by new and more powerful "centrales" (sugar mills).

A small but interesting book, *Down in Puerto Rico with a Kodak* gives the impressions of a New Haven, Connecticut businessman on a trip to Puerto Rico in January, 1898, just before the invasion.

> I do not believe it is possible, should this island be cut off from all communication with the outside world, that the inhabitants could be starved out, as they have all the food at their own doors necessary to sustain life.

He added that "nearly every vegetable known to civilization can be

At the end of the nineteenth century, nearly every vegetable known to civilization was grown on the island. The photo shows a scene from one of the numerous market places.

grown here," mentioning the cultivation at that time of rice, corn, Irish potatoes, white and red beans, and many fruits, especially the "delicious" oranges and bananas. He also mentioned that despite the cheapness of rum he did not see one drunken person in ten days, and he said he believed "there were fewer criminals on this island (then with a population of around one million) than in New Haven county alone." He wrote, "I was informed by all with whom I spoke on the subject that the island was quite free from crime and that one could ride by night or day all over the island without fear of molestation."

The Puerto Ricans too were proud of their towns. The plazas were well-kept. An accompanying photograph shows a view of the plaza at Mayaguez with its handsome houses and buildings as they existed at the end of the Spanish era.

"In former times many rural dwellers of the island cultivated a few acres of their own," later wrote one American, "But as the years went by this ceased. Small farmers were displaced, having themselves to join the agricultural workers."

In the Spanish days, coffee was a major crop, and Puerto Rican coffee was considered a gourmet product and was exported to Europe. Its cultivation covered about 40% of the land. Sugar accounted for only 15%, with the rest given over to fruits, tobacco, and cattle. For some years, during the last century, Spain had allowed the island to trade with nations friendly to Spain. The United States tariff

A view from the plaza at Mayaguez showing the handsome houses and buildings as they existed at the end of the Spanish era.

Cathedral and Plaza at Guaynabo. The American photographer in 1898 noted that the citizens were proud of their town, that the plaza was well-kept, and that it served as a playground for the children and a general resort for all the people.

laws abolished this. Since it was less profitable than sugar, no tariff protected the entry of Puerto Rican coffee around which three quarters of Puerto Rican rural life was centered, into the States. The permission from Spain allowing trade with Europe and islands of the Caribbean was accompanied by the right to buy and register foreign boats as Spanish. With the compulsion to use United States ships, the coffee export to New York became double the cost of shipping from Rio de Janeiro to New York which was twice the distance. Soon American companies owned most of the tobacco and fruit industries, and over 60% of the sugar plantations.

Sugar now became king, as in so many of the Caribbean islands, because it was most profitable. By 1902, thirty-nine sugar mills were controlling ⅛ of the total farm area. In one year it gave 115% profit to American owners. The sugar crop of 1897 of 72 thousand tons had reached 856 thousand tons in 1930, and yield per acre had risen three and a half times. The industry was also aided by the local government with the building of roads and irrigation projects, and help in experimentation. Home-produced food was no longer available, and reliance had to be placed on high-priced imported food from the American market. A diet of rice and beans and dried cod, when it could be afforded became prevalent throughout the island. This early change in Puerto Rico's economy was the root of much of the dislocation of its people and many of its future problems.

In 1897 Puerto Rico received 12,222,599 pesos for its coffee exports; 4,411,518 pesos for sugar and molasses; and 1,119,318 pesos for tobacco. Four years later 54.9% of its exports belonged to the sugar industry, followed by coffee with 19.6% and tobacco with 7.9%. By 1911 sugar had risen to 51.3% and tobacco to 17.4%, while coffee had been reduced to 12.5%.

Early in the twentieth century American sugar interests were already buying land and the trend was so alarming that there was a campaign urging Puerto Rican farmers not to sell their lands to foreign interests. The campaign failed. In 1903, Puerto Ricans owned 93% of the lands. In 1942, four American sugar companies were the owners of 52% of the land in Puerto Rico.

Cockfighting on the island and lotteries were forbidden when the Americans took over. Many of Puerto Rico's people were cockfighting fans. The government lottery, with profits going to education, indulges the dreams of all Puerto Ricans, then and now, who hope one day to be among the winners.

There was a positive as well as a negative side to the American occupation. However, this was achieved mostly in a later period and not in the initial four decades.

Under Spanish rule, villages were isolated and roads were poor. Though there are now good roads, isolated cottages and shacks still exist in the mountains. (PHOTO COURTESY OF THE DEPARTMENT OF AGRICULTURE.)

Traffic begins to build up outside all the towns at the rush hours: 8:30 a.m. and 4:30 p.m., the usual work period. (PHOTO BY MARTIN SAMOILOFF, JR.)

One of the hundreds of tropical trees at the Mayaguez Institute of Tropical Agriculture's Botanical Gardens. (PHOTO BY MARTIN SAMOILOFF, JR.)

Under Spanish rule, there were poor postal, telegraph, and cable services. There was a coach service, but the towns and villages were isolated and the roads were poor. The American administration improved roads and transportation, as well as the means of communication by telephone, telegraph service, and by the United States post offices. Thousands of miles of good roads had by a later date appeared all over the island. In fact, at the present time, there is so much congestion on the roads by automobile traffic especially during commuting hours, that "tapones," (traffic jams,) are part of the local scene around San Juan and other large cities.

The United States Forestry Department concerned itself with reforestation. The United States Agriculture Department operated experimental stations. The National Park Services helped preserve areas in Puerto Rico for recreation.

Another improvement was in the health of the island. One American "medico" who is greatly honored by Puerto Ricans is Dr. Bailey Ashford. He was responsible for controlling the devastating diseases of malaria and tuberculosis. San Juan now has several medical schools, hospitals in all the major towns, and health clinics in the smaller ones. The latter give free medical attention. Yet as in

Here are hundreds of small coffee trees ready to be shipped out from a nursery center grown on hill and mountainsides. (PHOTO COURTESY OF THE DEPARTMENT OF AGRICULTURE.)

education, where private education is good and public education poor, so it is so in the realm of medicine. The well-to-do obtain good care, the poor cannot afford the best facilities, nor often the worst.

Some medical instruction is now being given over the government station. This includes all aspects of hygiene, care of teeth, information about heart disease and cancer, and stresses the need of children to be inoculated against children's diseases. It is all told simply and graphically.

In 1898, there was a change for the better in education. There was a great growth in education. In the early 1800's, under Spain, there were only two public elementary schools, though some private schools existed. A secondary school was started in 1832, and a black had opened a school for his people in 1810. However, within fifty years the realization for the need for education had increased the number of public schools to 520 by the time of the American invasion. By 1910, this number was tripled and there were 1,687 public schools. However, the teaching was in English, which made it difficult for many children to learn in a foreign language. The change back to teaching in Spanish occurred in 1949.

Young coffee trees are sprayed against pests by Puerto Rican agriculturists. (PHOTO COURTESY OF THE DEPARTMENT OF AGRICULTURE.)

The early University of General Studies, St. Thomas Aquinas, started in San Juan in 1532 under the Spanish, had been transferred after a short while to Santo Domingo. Though this had been a frequent request from Puerto Ricans, Spain never established a proper university on the island. Since there was no local university, the sons of the wealthy went abroad, mostly to Spain, to get their degrees. The Ateneo Puertoriqueño, the oldest cultural agency on the island, did offer, ten years before the American arrival, courses in law and medicine and other subjects usually connected with a university. Earlier, in the middle of the century, a school had been organized by a Franciscan monk to teach the sciences. Eugenio de Hostos is Puerto Rico's most renowned teacher. He worked in education and wrote for it not only in his native land but in Santo Domingo and South America. Five years after the Americans arrived, the University of Puerto Rico was established. It was built in Rio Piedras on the outskirts of San Juan. The university has a pleasant campus with green lawns, great old trees, and a palm-lined entrance. Its main building with a clock tower is Moorish in design.

Since its early beginning, seventy-five years ago, the university has expanded its programs to include all the liberal arts and sciences as

Banana trees also are sprayed against pests. Note the "hand" of fruit on the left and the mountain range in the background. (PHOTO COURTESY OF THE DEPARTMENT OF AGRICULTURE.)

The Department of Agriculture has nurseries where the plants it has developed are sold at low cost. (PHOTO COURTESY OF THE DEPARTMENT OF AGRICULTURE.)

well as medical and law schools. There are now graduate programs given in economics, Spanish studies, chemistry, and public administration. The College of Agriculture and Mechanical Arts is situated in Mayagüez. The university's Nuclear Center is also here. The schools of medicine are located in San Juan and a two-year regional college is in Humacao.

The island also has a number of other universities and colleges. Inter-American University has two campuses—in San Juan and in San Germán. It is bilingual in its teaching. There is also the Catholic University of Puerto Rico as well as in Ponce. A World College in Bayamon and other regional colleges in different towns on the island. Today, there is much discussion of what a university should provide. There are those who think a university should be a place of learning in the widest sense and those who think it should be a place of learning in the narrow sense, that is, in offering training for specific jobs. All Puerto Ricans, however poor, and whatever their viewpoint, have a passionate desire that at least one of their children should have the advantage of a college education.

In general, the public schools in Puerto Rico are of low standard. The buildings are run down; the equipment poor; and the dropout rate is high, starting even before high school is reached.

Puerto Rico spends a third of her budget on education, one of the highest percentages in the world. Yet the schools on the whole, especially in rural districts, are below standard.

Another change that came with the new administration was in the area of religion. With the American entry, all forms of Protestanism appeared.

In regard to religion, today, as well as the original Anglican church in Ponce, there are Protestant churches throughout the island. A fine Episcopalian Cathedral can be visited in San Juan.

Among Protestants on the island are also Baptists and Jehovah Witnesses. Baptismal ceremonies can often be viewed on the beaches. The minister in white robes, with an assistant in blue robes, submerges clothed children and adults in the ocean. Later, another ceremony is held in a small tent erected on the "playa (beach). The churches of the Baptists and Jehovah Witnesses, in contrast to the Catholic Churches, are usually very simple wooden structures with plain crosses on the roofs. They are often in poorer districts, attended by the poor, and paid for and supported by them. Many are revivalist of the black-cult type, with much singing and hand-clapping.

Puerto Rico, however, is still mainly a Catholic country. Under American rule, the higher level Spanish or mulatto priests were replaced by Irish Catholic ones. The present archbishop is the first

Puerto Rican to be appointed head of the Catholic Church on the island. The Catholic Church and its ministers stand strongly for authoritarianism, and like their counterparts in other countries are anti-divorce and anti-abortion. However, some priests and clergy have become more progressive in recent years. Some are taking their stand with the "independentistas" and some stand for the political and social reforms.

In Spanish times, Puerto Rico had few roads, and a bare twenty kilometers of railroad track. The separation between town and countryside was sustained by medieval communication systems. Typically, Spain restricted her construction activities on the island to the building of a road system by her military engineers. The impressive Carretera Militia, linking the north and south coasts of the island across the crest of the central mountain range, was built by convict and imported Chinese labor. Chinese labor had been used since the building of El Morro Castle. Under American rule there was an improvement in the railroad lines and an increase in the number of good roads. However, the new road system developed in Puerto Rico after 1900 primarily catered to the transportation needs of the new American sugar company, as the main road in Spanish Puerto Rico had catered to the needs of the military.

The next change of fundamental importance came to Puerto Rico with the Jones Act. In 1917, the Jones Act was passed by the United States Congress. This was the second Congressional Act in regard to Puerto Rico. There was a measure enacted with the Jones bill which improved the Legislature in Puerto Rico, so that within both the Chambers of the Senate and House, members were to be elected by universal male suffrage. However, an American governor still had veto power over any bill that was passed. He also chose five members of the Cabinet, the remaining three being appointed by the President of the United States. Authority, therefore, still rested with an American executive within the island, while the overall authority still rested with the President and the U.S. Congress. All matters in regard to Puerto Rico were handled by the Bureau of Insular Affairs in the War Department.

There were other measures in the Jones Act of great importance. On the eve of the First World War, Puerto Ricans were given United States citizenship. This was not put to a vote. Automatically everyone became a citizen unless he or she signed a document refusing it. However, such a refusal deprived them of numerous civil rights, including the right to vote and the right to hold office. This really gave them no choice. It is difficult to know how many would have chosen American citizenship if there had been no restrictions. As it

A group of Puerto Ricans on the beach near Arecibo in 1898. In 1917, they became United States citizens.

was, all but a few handful did elect to become American citizens.

As citizens of the United States, Puerto Ricans fought in World War I and II, and in the Korean and Vietnam wars. Today, the U.S. military is the largest employer on the island, and recruitment recently has been stepped up. Boys joining the R.O.T.C. are given monthly stipends toward their college expenses. The local National Guard has also increased its numbers. For the unemployed, there is a strong attraction to join one or other of the military units.

Puerto Ricans could, from 1917 on, move freely from the island to the States. Many began to emigrate to look for work since unemployment was high at home. As citizens, they became eligible for welfare and social security (though these were lower than in the United States). Other further federal funds were also made available to them. In recent years this has been particularly true in regard to the Food Stamp program. Puerto Rico receives more aid than any state.

A column by Richard H. Boyce, in the *San Juan Star* of January 12, 1977, states that Puerto Rico now gets approximately $200 million a year in grants from Washington, mostly in welfare, education, and housing.

After the First World War, the new Puerto Rican Legislature again asked the U.S. Congress to put a vote to the people regarding independence. It was felt that the people should have a proper opportunity to decide on their own future. The call for a plebiscite was rejected. President Harding came out against Puerto Rican independence. The House Insular Affairs Committee Chairman wrote to the island legislature stating that there was no sentiment in the States for Puerto Rican independence and any hope for further measures of self-government would be injured by independence propaganda. The Secretary of War also stated to a Congressional Committee that "there was no sentiment whatever in the United States that the island of Puerto Rico should be an independent sovereignty, nor that it should not for all time be connected with the United States.

Most of the appointed governors were poorly equipped to deal with the problems of the island. They were all political appointees and none of them learned Spanish. They came and went—mediocre men at best. Between the two world wars, Puerto Rico was neglected. The island experienced terrible poverty. It became known as "The Pest Hole of the Caribbean." B. W. and J. W. Diffie wrote of "The Broken Pledge" in regard to the United States's commitment to their colony. They reminded Americans of Major General Nelson A. Miles' first promise to Puerto Rico:

> The people of the United States in the cause of liberty, justice and humanity . . . come bearing the banner of freedom, inspired by a noble purpose . . . [to] bring you the fostering arm of a nation of free people, whose greatest power is in justice and humanity to all those living within its fold. . . . to promote your prosperity, and to bestow upon you the immunities and blessings of the liberal institutions of our government.

The authors felt that promise had been sadly broken. They reminded their countrymen of what Theodore Roosevelt, Jr., one of the best governors of Puerto Rico, had written,

> Riding through the hills, I have stopped at farm after farm, where lean, underfed women and sickly men repeated again and again the same story—little food and no opportunity to get more.
>
> From these hills the people have streamed into the coastal towns, increasing the already severe unemployment situation there. . . . In

Theodore Roosevelt, Jr. wrote in the early years of American occupation, "I have seen as many as ten housed in a makeshift room not more than twelve feet square." Many Puerto Ricans still live in such shacks today.

some of the poorer quarters I have seen as many as ten housed in a makeshift room not more than twelve feet square.

I write now not what I have heard or read, but what I have seen with my own eyes, I have seen mothers carrying babies who were little skeletons. I have watched in a classroom, thin, pallid, little boys and girls trying to spur their brains to action when their little bodies were underfed. I have seen them trying to study on only one scanty meal a day, a meal of a few beans and rice. I have looked into the kitchens of houses where a handful of beans and a few plantains were the fare of the entire family.

The young Roosevelt wrote further on the health situation which had become deplorable over the thirty years.

His report went on:

We were and are a prey to disease of many kinds. In the fiscal year ending June 30, 1929, 4,442 of our people died from tuberculosis. Our death rate from this disease was higher than any other place in the Western hemisphere, and 4½ times the death rate in the Continental United States. Our death rate from malaria was 2½ times the rate in the Continental United States. Phrasing it differently, some 35,000 people in our island are now suffering from tuberculosis, some 200,000 from malaria and some 600,000 from hookworm . . .

In 1979 two-thirds of the population were below the poverty level and there are thousands of shacks like this one, which this old man calls home. (PHOTO BY PIPO GRAJALES, SAN JUAN STAR.)

> This condition is all the more deplorable because the climate here is exceptionally healthy. We have a moderate temperature varying little during the year. We have an abundance of sunshine. The trade winds blow through the majority of the year. We should be nearly free from such plagues as tuberculosis.

This gloomy assessment of conditions in Puerto Rico during the thirties was repeated by most other observers of the time.

Ironically, there were now more schools and hospitals. There was a Porto Rico Railway, a Light and Power Company, a Porto Rico Gas Company, a Porto Rico Telephone Company. There were large sugar plantations and tobacco and fruit industries. Even at this time there had been practically continuous investments of American capital in Puerto Rico according to a Brookings Institute report. Nevertheless, the condition of the people of Puerto Rico at this period was, from all reports, the bleakest in its history.

Rexford Guy Tugwell was to write of it as "The Stricken Land." Not until he was sent as governor by Franklin Roosevelt was the picture of the island, as a poor, forgotten, hurricane-ridden spot in the Caribbean, to change.

7
Modernization and Industrialization

MODERN Puerto Rico can be said to have had its birth in the forties. A new era began. This was the time when in 1941, Rexford Tugwell was sent to the island as governor by President Franklin D. Roosevelt. Tugwell was an able administrator—a member of the "Brain Trust." He was sympathetic to the island's problems. Fortunately, at the same moment, there was a Puerto Rican on the scene, who was historically one of the most charismatic of the island's leaders. This was Muñoz Marin, son of Muñoz Marin Rivera, who had been Resident Commissioner for Puerto Rico in Washington. Muñoz Marin therefore learned his politics in the American capitol, knew English well, and in his early days, with a felicity and facility for words, became a poet and editor of *La Democracia,* a paper founded by his father. Later this gift for words would enrich his powers as a compelling orator. He was also at first an "independentista," feeling strongly that Puerto Rico should be given its independence.

In 1940 he started a new party, Partido Popular Democratica (Popular Democratic Party—P.D.P. for short). He went into the hills, the villages, the rural areas, and all parts of the cities, asking the people to give him their votes and not sell them for two dollars apiece as they had in the past. He won their confidence and obtained their votes.

A modern sugar "central" (sugar mill) where the cane is brought to be cleaned and processed by modern machinery. Sugar is the basis for Puerto Rico's five rums. (PHOTO COURTESY OF DEPARTMENTO DE AGRICULTURA.)

As leader of the majority P.D.P. party, he worked closely with Tugwell. They were both men of imagination and capability. They both wanted to help mitigate the poverty and misery of the people.

First attempts at industrialization were made. These were "light", labor intensive industries. A bottle factory was founded to hold the rum from the sugar cane "centrals." Then a cement factory was started, so that small inexpensive houses could be built. The houses were to cost three hundred dollars each with a mortgage guaranteed by the government for twenty years. The village paid for the cement and necessary construction material for each house. The government supplied a supervisor and the men of the village provided the labor force on their leisure time. Each house had four rooms: kitchen-living room, bathroom, two bedrooms, and a small balcony facing the street. When all the necessary number of houses had been built, the old shacks were burnt and the village held a "fiesta." Everyone was enthusiastic about the new program which would wipe out slums.

The "cementos" were just one of the ideas of "Operation Bootstrap." This was a plan to improve the economy of the island

The "cemento" type housing first developed for the poor under the "Operation Bootstraps" conception of ex-Governor Muñoz Marin. (PHOTO COURTESY OF THE DEPARTMENT OF AGRICULTURE.)

Light industries from the United States are given ten to fifteen years free from taxes as an incentive to settle in Puerto Rico. (PHOTO COURTESY OF THE DEPARTMENT OF AGRICULTURE.)

through its own efforts. Puerto Rico was pulling itself out of its long-existing poverty. Light industries from the United States were given ten or fifteen years free from taxes as an incentive to start factories on the island to help overcome perpetual unemployment. Within a few years progress was evident. Puerto Rico became a "showcase" to be exhibited as an example to other undeveloped countries. Soon it was felt that the industries the government itself had launched should be sold to the private sector. Luis Ferré, a Puerto Rican businessman, was loaned money with which to buy the cement factory. Later he became a millionaire and governor of the island.

The Second World War brought a general economic upswing. Rum, which was more easily brought from Puerto Rico than Scotch was from the British Isles, gained in popularity in the States. The excise tax from the rum was returned to the island. Many Puerto Ricans also entered the U.S. Armed Forces and fought in all areas of the war. This helped to bring down unemployment.

Nevertheless, the general favorable financial picture did not include the poor majority. They still suffered. Food prices were unprecedently high because there was a food shortage. Unemployment remained high and there were many strikes in the factories.

After the war and the retirement of Rexford Guy Tugwell, Puerto Rico was given her first local-born governor, Jesús Tribio Pinero.

He was a student of Engineering who studied at the Universities of Puerto Rico and the University of Pennsylvania.

He helped found the Popular Democratic party which worked for social and economic reforms.

In 1946, President Truman appointed him governor of Puerto Rico. He worked for two major projects: the public ownership of utilities and the right of Puerto Ricans to elect their own governor.

On November 2, 1948, President Truman allowed Puerto Rico to elect its own governor. Muñoz Marin, by a large majority vote, became the first popularly elected governor of the island under the American administration. He was re-elected in 1952, 1956, and 1960. In 1949 for the first time since 1898, and after long popular demand, teaching in Spanish became the official policy of the schools with English a second language.

Muñoz Marin was a governor of enormous popularity. He was strongly supported by the "jibaros" of the hills and the rural areas. Their wide straw hat, the "pava" became the emblem of his party. He was also supported by the new lower-middle classes, whose growth had begun with the new industries and the creation of government services. For these Puerto Ricans, there were now city or suburban single home "urbanizations," housing developments, where the new generation, children of the rural poor, had such luxuries as washing machines and television sets. Then there were "caserios," blocks of apartments with low rents for poorer people. The city slums were also to be eliminated. All these people were ardent "Populares," and the P.D.P.'s red and white flag flew over the island. Its slogan was "Pan, Tierra y Liberdad" (Bread, Land, and Liberty).

Muñoz revived the political idea of an Associated Free State or Commonwealth. It was not "free" in the sense of being independent; neither was it a state. It was also not a commonwealth as generally understood, such as the Commonwealth of Massachusetts or any of the countries of the British Commonwealth. To many jurists, it was not even constitutional. The concept was interpreted to mean different things for different people. President Truman called it "a new relationship that will serve as an inspiration to all who love freedom."

The general idea of an Associated Free State was that Puerto Rico now would enjoy several further measures of self-government. A new constitution was drawn up and ratified by the United States Congress. Approved by the people and the Congress, Puerto Rico's Constitution was proclaimed on July 25, 1952. Puerto Rico was now allowed to fly its own flag beside that of the United States stars and stripes. It sang its own national anthem, *La Borinquēna,* as well as *The Star Spangled Banner.* But, the United States Congress can still override laws passed by the Puerto Rican Legislature.

Economically Puerto Rico has been developing since the beginning of the commonwealth era. Average annual income rose from about two hundred dollars in 1940 to two thousand dollars in 1977. In other spheres, too, there has been progress. Life expectancy rose during the same period from forty-eight years to seventy-six years. However, Puerto Rico's economy is closely tied to that of the United States. An economic boom in the States means a period of prosperity in Puerto Rico. A decline is reflected even more sharply on the island. A shift in priorities or changes in the economic policy of the United States is always felt on the island. Though there has been an economic improvement for the upper and middle classes, the poor, still the majority, have been left out of the mainstream of the developing modernization and economic growth. High-rise buildings, condominiums, and plush hotels now form the new San Juan. The metropolis has spread to include new suburbs with American type shopping centers and an outer ring of modern "urbanizations" to house about a third of the total population. But behind the fine modern buildings, the shacks of the poor are still to be found.

With the industrialization of the island and the setting up of the Economic Development Administration (Fomento) under the Com-

The lights of the modern buildings in San Juan are reflected in the waters of a lagoon. (PHOTO COURTESY OF PUERTO RICO INFORMATION SERVICE.)

monwealth, there has been an increase, as stated, in the national wealth. The Gross National Product now stands close to $7 billion. However, the wealth has not reached the wide mass of the people. About twenty-two per cent of the population live on two dollars a day; a further fourteen percent on three or four dollars a day. Roughly, a total of sixty-two percent of the families have an income under four thousand dollars a year. The Food Stamp program has been of great help, but it is a palliative, not a solution. Many blame the continuing grim situation on the fact that Puerto Ricans have too many children. But a recent study by two University of Puerto Rico professors shows that the birth rate now has only a low two percent annual growth. Information on birth control, free contraceptives, and sterilization services have been given since 1956 (against the opposition of the Catholic Church).

During the forties and fifties, there was an almost universal spirit of euphoria. The United States and Puerto Rico, working together, had attempted to solve the twin problems of poverty and colonialism. By the sixties, this sense of optimism was dying and by the seventies it was almost dead.

There was a change also in the course of "Fomento" and the "Popular" administration in the 1960s: a change from light to heavy industry. This was mainly illustrated by the construction of a petro-

A change from light to heavy industry, was undertaken with the construction of a petro-chemical complex. (PHOTO BY FRANK H. WADSWORTH.)

chemical plant on the south shore which was to have a chain reaction of "down-stream" industries. However, after the initial construction, the plant now employs few people. It consumes large quantities of the island's energy and causes considerable pollution. Bringing in refining crude oil from abroad continues but there have been no "spin-offs." When imported oil went up in price, there were losses in the refineries.

As well as tax exemptions, under Public Law #82, industries such as Union Carbide or P.P.G. receive a government subsidy of no less than $3,250,000 annually to cover their energy costs.

In regard to energy in the future, Puerto Rico could look to solar energy as a means of lessening dependence on fuel oil. This island has 360 days of sunshine a year.

Now there is also a good possibility that Puerto Rico may possess oil off its north shore. Studies show that there is a ninety percent chance of extracting large quantities of oil from offshore drilling extractions. The government has an agreement with Mobil, Shell, Exxon, and Continental Oil authorizing companies to extract two hundred thousand barrels of oil per day for a period of thirty years at an investment of four hundred million dollars.

Another untouched mineral resource is copper which is found in the mountains near Utuado. Interest in Puerto Rico's copper re-

The dramatic sixteenth hole of Cerromar Beach Hotel's championship-caliber golf course has cool ocean breezes to offer its players as well as a splendid view of the Atlantic. (PHOTO COURTESY OF PUERTO RICO TOURISM DEVELOPMENT.)

sources has been shown especially by Kennecott and American Metal Klimax. The actual mining has been resisted for many years because of ecological reasons. The current proposal is to form a Puerto Rican Mining Corporation by which Puerto Rico would be required to invest equally with the other two companies.

There are other mineral possibilities including even a little gold that the Spaniards may never have fully exploited.

Large numbers of U.S. 'Blue Chip' Companies as well as many of the multinationals have built factories in Puerto Rico. There are several large canning factories, such as for tuna fish, but the majority of the fleets from which the catch is brought are foreign. Many of the large banks, such as Chase Manhattan, have branches on the island, and many of the banks under Puerto Rican names are owned by the United States. The same is true of the supermarkets ("supermercados") such as Grand Union. "Pueblo" supermarkets equally big in size and numbers is American owned.

The hotel industry is important to Puerto Rico, bringing in a considerable percentage of the annual income. Until recently American Airlines owned the Americana Hotel and Eastern Airlines, the Dorado Beach and Cerromar Hotels. The hotels are as large and as modern as those in Miami. Casinos are licensed in most of the hotels and recently "one-armed bandits" have been introduced. These help to entice passengers from the big cruise ships which stop over in San Juan harbor.

The Holiday Inn marks the beginning of San Juan, Puerto Rico's Condado strip, a stretch of property as modern as Miami. Tourism is an important factor in the island's economy. (PHOTO COURTESY OF PUERTO RICO TOURISM DEVELOPMENT.)

Tourism is an important factor in the island's economy. As well as the big hotels, guest houses are now being built out on the island for those with more moderate incomes and a desire for a quieter milieu. It is estimated that the San Juan International Airport has well over one million passengers coming for a vacation in Puerto Rico and another million or more passing through to other points in the Caribbean or South. The airport is very modern and well-designed. In front of the airport is a long row of fountains jetting their spray high under arc lights. Before them, on tall white poles, are the flags of the many nations that enjoy the airport facilities—a first statement by Puerto Rico of itself as a historical and strategic center, with spokes spreading out to the United States, to South America, to Africa, and to Europe.

United States companies are enticed to Puerto Rico by various incentives. The foremost one is tax exemption for ten or more years.

There are also cheaper labor costs. The minimum wage in the States is $2.50 an hour. Only a few industries in Puerto Rico, such as hotels and restaurants, pay this rate, and then not to all their employees. Less than forty per cent, that is most industries, pay less than $1.40 an hour. In manufacturing industries, the average hourly earnings is 48% of the earnings in similar American industries.

In regard to a Puerto Rican's standard as a worker, Ex-Fomento

(Industrial Development) Administrator Teodoro Moscosco is quoted in a *New York Times* advertisement praising the high productivity of Puerto Rican labor as well as its relatively low costs. "The latest U. S. Census of Manufacturers found that a worker in Puerto Rico returns an average of $4.03 in value for every dollar of wages earned." In the States, it is roughly three dollars. According to the Planning Board, "The island's manufacturing sector rose (in labor productivity) at twice the rate of United States manufacturing during the 1967 to 1972 period."

In the seventies, the general world recession has had disastrous effects on Puerto Rico's economy. In the preceding years, unemployment was officially 10 or 11%. Actually, it was about double that: 20 to 22%, since those who had given up the task of finding work were not counted. With the recession, the official figures are 20 or 22%, but in reality close to 40%. In some towns, even official figures concede that it is ninety percent. In particular, rural workers have become unemployed.

A migration to the States to look for work, begun much earlier, grew in numbers over the years. Today almost a third of Puerto Rico's total population lives in the States. They are, however, different from the East European immigrants who arrived in the States around the beginning of the century and between the two World Wars. On the whole, Puerto Ricans in the States think of the island as their home and desire, when able, to return to it. Each year, too, a considerable number of Puerto Ricans enter the States as seasonal migrant workers in the fields of the Eastern seaboard; in the tobacco fields in Connecticut; in the apple orchards further north and in the tomato fields and peach groves in Florida and the South.

There is a regulatory agency on the island and in New York to look after the interests of these workers, but it is not wholly effective. There are also other agencies and organizations in New York and other big cities set up to help Puerto Ricans, confused in a land of foreign language and customs. The children have difficulties in school and the dropout rate is high. The adults have difficulties in the job market—especially those who speak no English. An official report of the U.S. Civil Rights Commission states that Puerto Ricans living in the United States are on the lowest rung of all minority sectors.

Yet, some do learn trades in the States, and return to Puerto Rico with skills they put to good use and which upgrade them in the Puerto Rican community.

The island is dependent both for its imports from and exports to the States. Differentiation in 1972 between imports and exports was a billion dollars in North American favor, and many of its exports are in reality components sent from the States, finished in Puerto Rico, and shipped back again. Puerto Rico is fifth, not far behind Canada and Great Britain, as an importer of American goods. It creates more than 250,000 jobs in the United States by the American products it buys and consumes.

We have spoken about the American-owned shopping centers. It is now more efficient and simpler to bring food in great containers from the States than to deal with a number of small island producers. This had led to a decline in raising local vegetables and fruits. The supermarkets sell California rice and Florida oranges. Coffee of gourmet quality was exported in the fifties, sixties, and early seventies. Today, the coffee plantations have been allowed to decline and Puerto Rico imports over half its coffee needs. To a reasonable extent, Puerto Rico could be self-sufficient in raising much of its own food, but the local farmers cannot compete with their giant rivals, and they have not been given the necessary governmental support. Agriculture has therefore fallen into decline. This agricultural decline affects sugar, coffee, and citrus fruits as well as chickens and meat. The decline is said to be continuing at the rate of three percent a year.

Local production accounts for less than one-fourth of citrus fruit consumption on the island. There is a move now to reverse the trend. This year the Agriculture Department will develop a citrus fruit industry in Puerto Rico.

Agriculture Secretary Herbierto Martinez said that his department will set aside 10,000 *cuerdas* of land in the southern part of the island for the growing of citrus fruits. Martinez emphasized, however, that the development of any citrus-fruit industry would be a slow process since five years must elapse before a tree begins to bear fruit.

"This is really a long-range agricultural project," he said.

Meanwhile, although citrus trees grow wild in many parts of Puerto Rico, their fruits are left to rot, while oranges, limes, and grapefruit are shipped in from California and Florida.

Also, experiments conducted through the University of Puerto Rico's agricultural experimental station, over a period of a year and a half, show that rice grown in Puerto Rico could prove cheaper than buying it from the United States. This would increase farmers' profits and put many people to work. Because Puerto Rico can produce two or three crops a year it would also avoid the high shipping costs. Finally, rice, a staple food of the people, could be brought down from its present level of twenty-seven cents a pound to twenty cents a pound. At the moment, Puerto Rico spends $70 million a year in importing rice, usually from California. An initial four thousand

The citrus industry has been neglected. Here is an orange tree. In many places, oranges, grapefruit, limes fall to the ground for want of picking and are left to rot. But in the supermarkets Florida and California citrus fruits are sold. (PHOTO COURTESY OF THE DEPARTMENT OF AGRICULTURE.)

acres put into rice production would in no way cut into the area in use for sugar, whose profits fluctuate from year to year.

Industrialism backed by the United States has been shown not to be the answer to Puerto Rico's problems. Heavy industry, in particular, has been a culprit in using more than its share of energy, causing much pollution, and providing few jobs. Light industries remain because of tax incentives. But labor unions are growing on the island and with increased labor costs, many of these firms are looking elsewhere. The neighboring island of the Dominican Republic is an easy transfer and there workers' wages are among the lowest in the Caribbean and in South America.

As everyone agrees, the present economic situation in Puerto Rico is lamentable, with little hope offered for any reversal in its downward trend.

What has happened to the island since "Operation Bootstrap" began and what is the present situation is well exemplified in the 1972 inaugural speech of Governor Hernandez Colon, now leader of the P.D.P. He painted this picture of his island:

La Perla, a poverty-stricken community along the waterfront of old San Juan: scene of Oscar Lewis's book La Vida (PHOTO BY FRANK H. WADSWORTH.)

Poverty in Puerto Rico

While some segments of our society enjoy growing progress, thousands upon thousands of Puerto Ricans languish in seemingly unending poverty. . . Rising costs of living reduce real salaries. Hopelessness pervades the countryside. The products of our soil no longer sustain our rural population . . . The poor in our cities as well as in the country still hope for a better life, but so far their hopes remained unfulfilled . . . thousands have had to emigrate, to abandon their homes, to uproot themselves from their communities in search of new opportunities outside of Puerto Rico. And many times, instead of finding the opportunities they sought, they have had to rely on public welfare . . . they have encountered prejudice and incomprehension. The unemployed and the migrants still hope for new opportunities here in Puerto Rico, but so far their hopes have remained unfulfilled. One-third of our families live in housing unfit for human habitation . . . crowded in filthy shacks, without sanitation and many even without potable water. Most of the poor live in wretched urban slums. Their children play in filth—bathe in contaminated water . . . breathe polluted air . . . sleep huddled on the floor. Our sick suffer . . . even for months before they receive treatment. Many die without receiving it.

With such a statement from the governor in 1972, there is no question about the condition of the poor—a majority—in Puerto Rico today. Over 100,000 families live in slums, half without water. More than 600,000 out of a population of less than three million live on welfare. Conditions did not improve under Hernandez Colon, despite his compassion.

When Romero Barcelo of the N.P.P. succeeded him as governor in 1976, he also stressed in his inaugural speech that the greatest problems in Puerto Rico today are the widespread poverty, poor health, unemployment, and inadequate schools. All agree that despite gains in some sectors, the vast majority of Puerto Ricans remain poor and the fundamental cause is high unemployment. This in turn has led to a high and rising crime rate. The two are always related. A man without a job or money gets desperate and steals.

Operation Bootstrap, the economic development program launched in 1947, has lured over two thousand firms to the island by offering tax holidays and cheap labor forces. Unemployment, nevertheless, is now higher than it was when the program began.

In 1982, after President Reagan's cuts in social welfare programs, the plight of the majority of the people is dire. Previously, two-thirds of all the families on the island were receiving food stamps. Now this figure has been considerably lowered. Federal slashes made in other areas have also had a deleterious effect on the economic situation of the island.

The Island government is near bankruptcy. Both individual and company bankruptcies have risen greatly during the last year. Many smaller businesses have moved to countries where wages are lower. This has led to still further increases in unemployment. The official figure is 21 percent; the unofficial one is double that figure. Unemployment, then, is the major problem. The Economic Development Company of Puerto Rico (Fomento) is advertising in U.S. newspapers and periodicals for new plants under the slogan "The Ideal Second Home for American Business." Companies are not being asked to move their main plants to the island and so take away jobs in the States, but are being encouraged to move one part of the production process to Puerto Rico. Since Puerto Rican plants are tax-free in most cases, this suggestion has great appeal. Most of the large U.S. pharmaceutical firms have opened plants on the island and have found them very profitable.

Still, with economic woes mounting, the political situation in Puerto Rico, which until now has been relatively stable, could rapidly change.

8

Political Parties

WITH the coming of Americans in 1898, there were new political parties, but it was mostly a matter of changing names rather than changing policies and goals. The Partido Federal (Federal party), was founded a few months after Americans landed, while the island was still under military control. It was headed by Luis Muñoz Rivera and called for general suffrage, local autonomy, and similar concessions to those that Puerto Rico had gained from Spain in the previous year.

The Republican party, headed by Dr. José Celso Barbosa and Roberto H. Todd, was incorporated into the Republican party of the United States. The GOP has since supported *statehood* for Puerto Rico in many of its platforms, particularly in recent years.

The "Republicanos" was an assimilationist party desiring to become a part of the United States. Its platform included demands to all the rights of the states except that of sending representatives to Congress. This was a break from the tradition of sending representatives to the Spanish Cortés.

The "Federales" won in the 1899-1900 election but boycotted the elections that took place after the Foraker Act in 1900 since they felt that Washington was overwhelmingly on the side of the "Republicans." The "Republicanos" therefore won the first election under United States's administration. The "Liga de Patriotas Puertorriquēnos" was created by José de Hostos, who wanted a plebiscite held on the question of independence. When he found that the other parties were prepared to collaborate with the United States, he went into exile in the Dominican Republic until he died.

In the years between 1900 and 1917, there was considerable friction in the Puerto Rican Congress between those selected by the United States and those elected by Puerto Rico. One of the major points of friction was the management of funds. Also, during these years, Puerto Ricans continued to agitate for greater control over their own destinies, and independence remained a plank of the Unionist party, though it was not sought very vigorously.

During this time, Teddy Roosevelt put forward his famous corollary to the Monroe Doctrine, which was thus extended to mean that not only must European powers be kept out of the Western Hemisphere, but that the United States had a right to intervene within the whole area. This was the policy of the "big stick," which was not well-received in South America nor in Puerto Rico. It crushed all hopes of any legal and formal progressive steps towards independence.

For the 1904 election, Muñoz Marin Rivera founded a new party called Partido Union de Puerto Rico. By calling for unity on the three forms of status, it won the next eight elections from 1904 to 1924 (Muñoz Marin Rivera went as Puerto Rico's representative to Washington in 1910.) El Partido Union de Puerto Rico was middle of the road in ideology, wide enough in its platform to include those for independence, those for statehood, and those for greater reform and self government—the "autonomistas."

In later years, interestingly enough, those who similarly campaigned as the Union party—men such as Muñoz Marin, Luis Ferré, and Romero Barcelo, saying status was not the issue, gained majority support as the Union party had done.

Since most of the Union members had been Federalists, they called for more self-determination for the island, named their newspaper *La Democracia,* and were loosely tied with the Democratic party of the States.

The first independence party under the new regime was not formed until 1912 and was short-lived. The first Socialist party was formed in 1915, linked weakly with the Socialist party of the States. Its leader was Santiago Iglesias, and it was essentially a workers' party, a trade union party, with only mild socialist ideas.

The Unionist party first advanced the idea of a "Commonwealth." This was the conception that Muñoz Marin was to put into practice with the creation in the 1940s of his Partido Democratica Puertorriqueña (P.D.P.). The idea in the twenties, however, split the Unionist Party which had until then held power for nearly twenty years. The members of the party who were for independence, broke away to form the National party, calling without equivocation for a free, sovereign, independent Republic. By 1930, the party became more militant under the leadership of Pedro Albizu Campos.

Puerto Rico had a government of its own at the time of the invasion, 1898. Yet, it was not asked to participate in, nor to ratify the Paris Treaty. Pedro Albizu Campos, the Nationalist leader of the 1930s and the fifties claimed that the treaty was invalid as far as the island's inhabitants were concerned.

Another party for independence, besides the Nationalists, The Movimiento Pro-Independencia (M.P.I.) was reorganized in November 1959 under the name of Partido Socialista Puertorrinqueño (P.S.P.) and was openly Marxist though not associated with the Communist party. The Partido Independentista Puertorrequeño (P.I.P.) had been founded in July, 1948 under the leadership of Dr. Gilberto Concepción de Gracia. The party wanted to obtain independence by peaceful means, but was not associated with the Nationalists. Later, under the younger leadership of Ruben Berrios, it added socialism to its planks, but continued to reject violence as a means to its

Juan Mari Bras (left) leader of the Partido Socialista Puertorriqueño (Puerto Rican Socialist Party) speaking over the radio, while another Puerto Rican independence leader, Ruben Berrios of the Partido Independencia Puertorriqueño, (P.I.P) listens. Note the typical guayabera *shirts worn by both men.* (PHOTO JOSÉ GARCIA, SAN JUAN STAR.)

Ruben Berrios, addresses a crowd during the 1976 campaign.

goal. A Communist Party, formed in 1934, has always remained a very small party on the island. There are also other small groups that differ in one way or another from the two main parties of the P.S.P. and the P.I.P., but who support the cause for independence. Youth has been in the forefront of the new wave for independence. In the University of Puerto Rico, their forces are strong in the Federación de Universitarios Pro Independencia (F.U.P.I.). During the Vietnam War, many young Puerto Rican "independentistas" refused to be drafted, and they succeeded in having the R.O.T.C. conduct its exercises outside the campus.

There is also a Christian group for socialism and independence, which consists of both laymen and clergy, Protestant and Catholic. In all elections, the independence parties have shown small results. Yet their influence is much wider than this would indicate. The newspaper of the P.S.P., *CLARIDAD,* until recently a daily, had 100,000 subscribers for its special issues.

Essentially, the question of its status continued: as it had done

In the 1950s, the early days of industrialization of Puerto Rico, Governor Muñoz Marin is shown the modern machinery to be used for the processing of feed for cattle. (PHOTO COURTESY OF U.S. DEPARTMENT OF AGRICULTURE.)

under Spanish rule that is whether Puerto Rico should retain ties to the colonial metropolis while seeking greater local autonomy and self-government; whether it should be completely assimilated into the structure Spain in the past and of the United States in the present; or whether it should be completely independent.

Muñoz Marin, as had the Unionist party before him, suggested putting the question aside and concentrating on the economic betterment of the island. He put forward again the idea of "Commonwealth," or as it was also now to be called Estado Libre Associado (Free Associated State) and formed the new party of the "Populares" of the P.D.P. (Popular Democratic Party-Partido Democratica de Puerto Rico).

Unlike on the earlier occasion, many "independentistas" accepted the idea of Estado Libre Associado (E.L.A.) and flocked to the banner of the "Populares" believing it would lead them on a slow, nonrevolutionary road to independence after economic betterment. Others, however, swung over to the Nationalist party still under the leadership of Pedro Albizu Campos, a black Harvard graduate and an ex-officer in the U.S. army. They opposed Muñoz Marin, believing Commonwealth would lead to statehood rather than to independence.

The Nationalists decided to take direct action. On October 30, 1950, uprisings began in many towns as they had at the time of "Grito de Lares." The Nationalists occupied the town of Jayuya, which they held for three days and again the Republic of Puerto Rico was proclaimed. The house of Pedro Albizu Campos was surrounded by police, but he would not surrender until learning of the collapse of the revolt. He was sentenced to fifty-three years in prison in a United States jail.

Nationalists also, as part of the insurrectionary call for independence, attacked Blair House in Washington where President Truman was living at the time. One of the President's guards was killed and one was wounded. One of the revolutionaries was killed and another wounded. Severe repressions were taken against the Nationalists both in Puerto Rico and in the States. Their sympathizers were rounded up and thrown into jail. Another action to draw world attention to Puerto Rico's cry for independence was on March 1, 1954, when five Nationalists, one of them a woman, fired shots from the Visitors' Gallery in the House of Representatives in Washington, wounding five members. All were immediately arrested and given long jail sentences. A Blair House attacker and the three House disturbers remained in American prisons for twenty-three years until they were released in 1979. All Puerto Rican parties, sympathetic or unsympathetic to the independence cause had been trying to obtain their release.

Early in the year of 1952, a Constitutional Convention was held. The proposed Constitution was then put to a popular referendum. The document, which needed United States approval, included a resolution that read:

> The people of Puerto Rico reserve the right to propose and to accept the modifications in the terms of its relation with the United States of America, in order that these relations may at all times be an expression of an agreement freely entered into between the people of Puerto Rico and the United States of America.

The referendum of the proposed Constitution was approved by 374,649 and rejected by 82,923 Puerto Ricans. Some did not participate.

The proposed Constitution was then put before the United States Congress. The Congress deleted the Bill of Rights section that had been included. These rights had been for education, for employment, for a fair standard of living and for other measures similar to those included in the American Bill of Rights. The Congress, while ratifying the Puerto Rican Constitution in 1952 with these deletions, also amended it with a statement that there would be no relinquishing of United States plenary powers over the island. This meant that the Puerto Rico Constitution and its Congress would be subject to that of the United States. Puerto Rico became a Commonwealth on July 25, 1952. It has become an annual holiday called Constitution Day.

After the actions of the Nationalists in the fifties, the independence movement was muted, not to rise strongly again for nearly a decade. Then again, it began to play a part in Puerto Rican politics, under new leadership, new political parties, and new directions.

The Commonwealth concept had a long period of acceptance by the Puerto Rican people. But by the sixties, the idea was being questioned. The Statehood party began to gather strength. Muñoz Marin realized this threat to his party, the P.D.P., and as a means of combating the political competition, tried to get more concessions of autonomy from the United States Congress. He was unsuccessful.

Though still immensely popular, still a charismatic figure, after sixteen years as governor he voluntarily stepped down from office. From that time on the fortunes of the P.D.P. began to wane. The "Commonwealth," the "Bootstrap Operation" which had offered so much promise and which had accomplished much in the beginning,

Muñoz Marin addresses a crowd of well-wishers outside a house dedicated to his statesman father, Luis Muñoz Rivera.

Don Luis Muñoz Marin is given bunches of flowers by his admirers during a birthday celebration.

did not seem to be solving the basic social and economic problems of the island. "Fomento" (the Economic Development Corporation) brought over 2,000 United States companies to the island by its offer of "no taxes" incentive. The companies included multinational and two hundred "Blue Chip" corporations. However, unemployment was still rife. Though a new middle class had arisen which had benefited from industrialization, the majority remained poor and outside the modern mainstream. Muñoz Marin had tried to obtain an improvement in the Commonwealth status from the Federal Government, but Congress opposed giving the island greater sovereignty.

Muñoz was followed as governor by his chosen successor, Roberto Sanchez Vilella. During his term a Commission was set up by Washington to study the status question. This plebiscite resulted from an earlier agreement between Muñoz Marin and President John F. Kennedy. After its findings had been made public the next year, a plebiscite took place, the first referendum on status in Puerto Rico. Sixty-five percent of the people voted. The results in round figures were 400,000 for Commonwealth, 275,000 for statehood, and only 4,250 for independence. The "independentistas" had mainly abstained from voting. The results meant continuing a middle-of-the-road position for the island in regard to status. During President Lyndon Johnson's term in office, another status commission was formed. It had an American chairman and six other Americans, including two university professors, one Democrat and one Republican. On the Puerto Rican side, there were also six representatives; two P.D.P.er's, one from the Popular party, two statehooders, and one independence supporter. All of them were appointed by Governor Muñoz Marin. But Dr. Concepcion de Gracia withdrew from the commission stating that the alternative of independence was not being given objective consideration.

Toward the end of Vilella's first term, he divorced his wife of long-standing to marry a younger woman. Though this is a very frequent occurrence in Puerto Rico, in this instance the women of Puerto Rico were up in arms over the matter. In the face of strong voter opposition, Sanchez Vilella said he would not seek a second term. However, when the time arrived, and another P.D.P. gubernatorial candidate was chosen, Vilella decided to run against him. To do so, he formed a new party, the Popular party, thus causing a split in the P.D.P. ranks. This led to its defeat in the 1968 elections, though the P.D.P. and the Popular Party vote together presented a majority.

Louis Ferré, an industrialist, had run in the election of 1964 as a candidate for statehood for the Partido Estadista (Republicano). He gained 30% of the votes, while Vilella, his opponent on the P.D.P. ticket garnered 60 per cent. For the second contest, Ferré formed a new party, one with a broader basis than the statehood issue. This was the Partido Nuevo Progresista (New Progressive party), organized in 1967. Though many of its members were "statehooders," this was not the main plank of the new party. It still kept its ties with the G.O.P., the Republican Party of the United States.

In 1972, the NPP lost out again to the P.D.P. Its new leader, Hernandez Colon, a young, energetic man, faced tasks as a politician, based on economics, which were almost insolvable within his party's framework. For most Puerto Rican people, there was a strong conviction that their earlier expectations were not being realized. This feeling was expressed in Hernandez Colon's own inaugural speech of 1972. The United States and world recession, which hurt Puerto Rico badly, occurred during his term of office. This strengthened the common feeling of lost hope. Hernandez Colon, with the help of Jaimé Benitez, ex-Chancellor of the University of Puerto Rico, and ex-Resident Commissioner in Washington, together with Muñoz Marin, formed, in conjunction with a group of United States delegates, and with President Ford's assent, an Ad Hoc Committee. There were seven Americans and seven Puerto Ricans: only one was a "state-hooder," and there was no representative of the independence point of view. The purpose of the Ad Hoc Committee

·Governor Hernandez Colon waves to the crowds as he commences post-1972 address, when he was still governor.

was to consider again the possibilities of increased autonomy. After fourteen months and many changes, a final draft was adopted and given to President Ford.

In the 1976 elections, the P.D.P. lost by a small percentage. It also lost its majority in the Puerto Rican Congress and in most municipalities throughout the island. The independence parties, though gaining votes, made a poor showing, losing their one Senator and two Representatives. The workers had, in great numbers, moved away from the P.D.P. but entered the N.P.P. ranks and not those of the independence parties, as the latter had hoped. Romero Barcelo, running for the governorship on the N.P.P. ticket, promised that statehood would not be an issue, offered a "Populist" program, and wrote a book, *Statehood Is For the Poor*. He won and is the present

Governor Hernandez Colon, among a group of schoolchildren during the 1976 election campaign, when he was running as a candidate.

Governor Hernandez Colon of the Partido Democratica Puertorriqueño (P.D.P) explains plans to a group of administrators in the Department of Agriculture. (PHOTO COURTESY OF THE DEPARTMENT OF AGRICULTURE.)

Governor of Puerto Rico, Carlos Romero Barcelo, who is an advocate of Statehood for the island.

governor. He now had to try to overcome Puerto Rico's social and economic problems.

In the 1976 elections, the dismal state of the economy, the high price of food, the inflation and the high unemployment finally defeated the P.D.P. There was the growing feeling that despite its rosy promise of the forties and fifties, it had since proved unable to solve the island's problems. Statehood or Independence again were being offered as the only alternatives. During the elections, there were television debates among all four candidates: Hernandez Colon for the P.D.P., Romero Barcelo for the N.P.P., and the two candidates who were running on tickets for independence. The young, good-looking Harvard-trained Ruben Berrios for the Partido Independentista Puertorriqueño (P.I.P.) was acknowledged by the newspapers and the general public to have been the most charismatic and the most effective speaker. Juan Mari Bras put forward with passion his party's socialist point of view, Partido Socialista Puertorriqueño (P.S.P.).

Of then present governor and the question of status, Andrew Viglucci, former vice-president of the *San Juan Star,* and a Pulitzer Prize winner wrote in 1973, "There are many who are pinning their hopes for Puerto Rico and for Statehood on Romero Barcelo, and there are possibly just as many who are dreading the day when he might succeed to the highest office of the island. There is a good chance that he . . . will be the person to force Puerto Rico into a confrontation with itself over status."

Romero Barcelo was not yet in office, when Gerald Ford in his last days as President, startled the United States and Puerto Rico by putting forward a bill to make the island the fifty-first state. He included no provision for Puerto Ricans to make a choice. The new President, Jimmy Carter, however had stated that Puerto Ricans would be consulted. Whatever their wishes, the final decision will be in the hands of the United States Congress, and by extension, in the hands of the American people. A poll taken just after President Ford's announcement showed fifty-nine percent of Americans being in favor of Puerto Rico's becoming the fifty-first state. A later poll by the *New York Daily Mirror* showed considerably less support for the idea. No poll was taken in Puerto Rico. President Ford had asked the Office of Management to evaluate the Ad Hoc Committee's recommendations for greater autonomy, while Puerto Rico waited to hear of his acceptance or rejection of the "new compact." However, he made no move on the recommendations and, unknown to the Ad Hoc Committee, had also asked the Office of Management for "other options." The other option was Statehood. The State Department had already made this its own choice. One high official, C. Arthur Borg, has written a study entitled, "The Problem of Puerto Rico's Political Status." He wondered in his booklet how far the United States could politically and constitutionally allow Puerto Rico greater autonomy. "Whether we are really prepared to support Commonwealth status in perpetuity, or whether we must prepare now for eventual statehood or independence." Another State Department officer felt that strategically and because of U.S. large economic and financial interests, Puerto Rico could not by itself be allowed to determine its own status.

Romero Barcelo had insisted in his campaign that status was not an

Old and new San Juan. The ancient blue paving stones, brought in as ballast in Spanish ships in the foreground; the San Juan Post Office, cars, a piragua *man in the right corner; a modern parking building in the background; and behind that Puerto Rico's* Capitolio *(Capitol), the Congressional building.* (PHOTO BY MARTIN SAMOILOFF, JR.)

issue, and it was on that understanding that he was elected. Just before the new governor's inauguration however President Ford made his proposal for statehood for Puerto Rico. This was followed on January 14, 1977, by President Ford's offering to Congress his Puerto Rico Statehood act.

The main points are:

1. The establishment of a Puerto Rico statehood commission—to hold hearings, conduct studies, and secure information from Federal agencies.
2. The commission will have five members appointed by the President of the United States and five members appointed by the present "statehooder" governor.
3. The commission will submit the final report to the President,

and to the Governor of Puerto Rico who will make public the document.
4. It provides by the U.S., its staff, and compensation and authorizes the commission to use the facilities of the Executive Branch of the Federal government.
5. The President and Congress determine if, in the light of the report, any additional action is necessary concerning the terms of Puerto Rico's admission as a state.
6. Following the above action, a referendum will be held, and if passed, a convention of delegates must be held for the adoption of the United States Constitution and the framing of a state government constitution.
7. The State Constitution voted on by the Puerto Ricans, will then be certified by the President and the United States Congress. The suggested time over which these steps would take place would be forty months.

Some additions to the original draft were adopted after consultation with Governor Romero Barcelo. The additions emphasized that Puerto Rico would have a say in her own destiny. However, the decision must rest finally, under the United States Constitution, with the United States Congress, and with the American people.

In the States, most Americans find Puerto Ricans strange and foreign. Few have any knowledge of the island or its history. Many are only vaguely aware of where the island is situated. Thousands of American tourists *do* flock to Puerto Rico in the winter and there is a brisk airline traffic especially between New York and San Juan. However, the tourists tend to find their amusements in the big hotels where they stay, coming in contact with very few Puerto Ricans except waiters, maids, and croupiers.

President Carter had said he will support whichever status Puerto Ricans prefer. A stated intention by the United States to hold a plebiscite on Puerto Rican status in 1981 may forestall the possibility of Puerto Rico's being named a colony by the United Nations.

The United Nations has occupied a role in United States-Puerto Rican affairs since 1952. Before that time, the United States was supposed to give an accounting to the world body on the territories and colonies under its guardianship. After the founding of the Commonwealth and a plebiscite in its favor, it was decided that such an annual report was no longer necessary. At a session of the General Assembly in 1953, in the debate on Puerto Rico's status, Henry Cabot Lodge, Jr., then United States Ambassador to the U. N. stated: "The United States is proud of its new relationship with Puerto Rico. . . . While, of course, I strongly favor the new status of Puerto Rico as a self-governing commonwealth associated with the United States . . . I

The flag that the Commonwealth Legislature Assembly adopted in 1952 as official emblem of Puerto Rico is an ancient flag designed by a group of patriots in 1895.

am authorized to say in behalf of the President (Eisenhower) that if, at any time, the Legislative Assembly of Puerto Rico adopts a resolution in favor of more complete or even absolute independence, he will immediately thereafter recommend to the Congress that such independence be granted."

The question of Puerto Rico was not raised again in the U. N. until recently. Then in 1972 and again in 1973, it agreed that its Decolonization Declaration of 1960 (Resolution 1514 IV) applied to Puerto Rico, and since that time it has kept the relationship of the island and the United States under continuous review. The United States has contended that this is "an internal affair."

Carlos Romero Barcelo, has said he would not defend "Commonwealth" status in the U. N., since, he says, the present relationship with the United States does "have some vestiges of colonialism." He has also stated that he believes statehood would win in a plebiscite. He adds that if Puerto Rico were asked to give up

Spanish as its main language and give up its Spanish culture, which he thinks the United States Congress will not ask, then he would opt for independence. (A somewhat similar request was made by New Mexico when it was incorporated into the Union.) If this were the case, Hernandez Colon is reported to have said that he, too, would choose independence. This may be mere rhetoric on the part of both men. The United Nations, and the Third World in particular, *do* consider the question a relevant one to be discussed in the world body. This view is supported by the island's parties for independence and the Popular Democratic Party as represented by Hernandez Colon.

The Puerto Rican Bar Association also recommends that the United States Congress transfer all power over Puerto Rico to the "Puerto Rican people" and that a constituent assembly draw up a "final solution" to the status problem.

The report on the "Decolonization of Puerto Rico" was written by twelve lawyers of the Association's Constitutional Law Commission, and approved by the governing board.

Association President, Graciana Miranda Marchand said that the "Puerto Rican people have developed a political maturity to resolve the colonization problem."

The Bar Association's function in the report is legal, not political, Miranda Marchand said, because it recommends the process for determining status, not what that status should be.

Citing a 1963 Association report, the new report recognizes three forms of status—independence, statehood, or association. In each of these, however, Puerto Rico should be the sovereign "ultimate source of power."

The report establishes some prerequisites to achieve decolonization. They are as follows:

1. All proposals should be made by the Puerto Rican people, free of external influence.
2. Congress should transfer sovereign power to Puerto Rico.
3. An interim government with all existing legal and constitutional structures should be recognized.
4. Decolonization should be supervised by the United Nations, at the island's request.
5. A Constitutional Assembly should be elected, and each status formula represented according to the votes cast.
6. The Assembly should conduct politics, social and economic studies, and should then submit a proposed constitution to the Puerto Rican voters.
7. Total amnesty should be given to Puerto Rican political prisoners.
8. The interim government should find alternatives to United

States military bases and federal aid which would guarantee "the freedom of determination."
9. A referendum will approve the final solution. Only those born in Puerto Rico, or resident children of Puerto Rican parents, can vote. No economic pressures should be put on the island to influence people's voting.

The report was written by lawyers representing the four major political parties. In many ways, it reflects the present position of the United Nations Decolonization Committee's views.

TEXT OF U.N. RESOLUTION

Following is the text of the resolution approved September 12, 78 by the United Nations Decolonization Committee. Ten nations voted for the resolution which was introduced by Cuba and Iraq; none voted against, but 12 abstained and two were absent for the voting.

The Special Committee

Having heard and considered the statements of the petitioners, which reflect the views of major trends of political opinion in Puegto Rico,

Recalling its resolution of 28 August 1972 and 30 August 1973, as well as its decision of 7 September 1976, concerning Puerto Rico,

Bearing in mind the decision on Puerto Rico adopted by the Conference of Foreign Ministers of the Co-ordinating Bureau of non-aligned Countries held in Belgrade in 1978 and by the Fifth Conference of Heads of State of Government of Non-Aligned Countries held at Colombo in 1976,

Conscious of the right of the people of Puerto Rico to modify the present status of Puerto Rico and aware that proposals for such modification have been made in the past by official organs of Puerto Rico,

Bearing in mind the Declaration on the Granting of Independence to Colonial Countries and Peoples contained in General Assembly resolution 1514 (XV) of 14 December 1960,

Conscious also that all peoples have the inalienable right to self-determination and independence, to the exercise of their national sovereignty, to respect for integrity of their national territory and to the exercise of complete control over their natural wealth and resources in the interest of their development and well-being,

Recalling the statement on Puerto Rico made on behalf of the United States of America by the permanent representative of the United States to the United Nations to the 8th session of the General Assembly on 27 November 1953,

Noting the public statement on Puerto Rico made by the President of the United States on 25 July 1978 and by the permanent representative of the United States on 28 August 1978.

Bearing in mind the fact that in their statements the petitioners have demonstrated that the major parties in Puerto Rico favor a change in the present status of Puerto Rico or modification of aspects thereof,

1. Reaffirms the ineliable right of the people of Puerto Rico to self-determination and independence in accordance with General Assembly resolution 1514 (XV);

2. Reaffirms that by virtue of that right the people of Puerto Rico should freely determine their future political status and pursue their further economic, social and cultural development;

3. Affirms that self-determination by the people of Puerto Rico in a democratic process should be exercised through mechanisms freely selected by the Puerto Rican people in complete full sovereignty in accordance with General Assembly Resolution 1514 (XV), which, inter alia, establishes the complete transfer of all powers to the people of the territory and that all determinations concerning status should have the approval of the Puerto Rican people,

4. Considers that the persecutions, harassments and repressive measures to which the organizations and persons struggling for independence have been continuously subjected constitute violations of the national rights of the Puerto Rican people to self-determination and independence;

5. Deems that in the event the Puerto Rican people decide to form an independent republic, they have the right to recover the totality of their territory including all lands now used by the authorities of the Government of the United States.

6. Deems also that any form of free association between Puerto Rico and the United States must be in terms of political equality in order to comply fully with the provisions of the relevant resolutions and decisions of the General Assembly and of applicable international law, and must recognize the sovereignty of the people of Puerto Rico;

7. Urges the Government of the United States to release unconditionally the four Puerto Rican political personalities who have been incarcerated for more than 24 years;

8. Urges the Government of the United States to abide by the principles of resolution 1514 (XV) with respect to Puerto Rico;

9. Decides to keep under review the question of Puerto Rico and requests the Rapporteur, with the assistance of the Secretariat, to update information on this question in order to facilitate consideration of appropriate follow-up steps by the Special Committee in 1979.

The United States has rejected the United Nations Decolonization Committee resolution calling for a complete transfer of powers to Puerto Rico before the island's people decide on their final political status.

"The United States has never recognized the jurisdiction of the

(Decolonization) Committee of 24 over Puerto Rico," said a spokesman for the U. S. State Department. 'Anything relating to the future status of Puerto Rico would have to emerge from the constitutional processes of the U. S. government and the government of Puerto Rico.'

One way or another, though, there will likely be changes in the relationship between Puerto Rico and the United States. President Carter had stated that he would be ready to accept the final decision made by Puerto Rico in a post-1980 referendum. U. N. Ambassador Andrew Young had granted approval for United Nation observers to oversee such a referendum. Meanwhile in Puerto Rico, the whole issue has become highly inflamed, highly partisan, and highly emotional, with leaders of all parties and other political figures giving different interpretations of the U. N. resolution.

Except for Henry Cabot Lodge's statement that Puerto Rico would be given independence if she wished, when the new concept of Commonwealth was put before the United Nations in 1953, the United States government has otherwise shown itself against this conception. The early American governors of the island, all expressed themselves forcefully against independence. President Harding was only one of many presidents proclaiming a similar attitude.

Vincenzo Petrullo, an adviser to government agencies, writing a book, *Puerto Rico Paradox,* in 1947 to promote understanding between Americans and Puerto Ricans, said:

> "Since 1898, when Puerto Rico was acquired by the Treaty of Paris, our policy has inclined towards the complete assimilation of its people, with full citizenship, though it has never been so stated officially."

Indeed, from the beginning, the United States has seen statehood for Puerto Rico as the final step in its possession of the island, as General Wilson, the first military governor, said:

> Puerto Rico will first be governed by a military regime; then it will be declared an American territory, and later it will achieve the category of sovereign state within the Union. The duration of these periods will depend more or less upon the merits of the country.

From time to time in the intervening eighty years, this same sentiment has been repeated by American authorities. Both the Republican and Democratic parties have had planks in their platforms in recent years for statehood for the island.

The Independentistas *of all parties will fight against any plebiscite on Puerto Rico's status alternatives unless Puerto Rico is first given sovereignty. Puerto Ricans are passionately interested in their political future. Here Ruben Berrios mingles with a group of young women working in a nearby factory.*

In the 1980 Puerto Rican elections, the N.P.P. gained forty-six percent of the votes, but part of this was a vote for change rather than for statehood. The P.D.P. Party obtained forty-four percent of the vote. With the independence vote, those against statehood are then still a majority. With these figures both the "Populares" and "Independentistas" say that the plebiscite for statehood will be defeated. This would only be if they were united. There will be many who will boycott the plebiscite. Senator Henry Jackson had declared that if the results show only fifty-one percent voting for statehood, this would be sufficient for the United States Congress's acceptance. (The voting in the plebiscite may well include American residents on the island and Cuban refugees who have become American citizens.)

The "Independentistas" will fight against the plebiscite, unless Puerto Rico is first given sovereignty. There may be violence as there was by the Nationalists after the earlier plebiscite for Commonwealth. Yet, there was until recently an underlying sense of inevitability among many Puerto Ricans, even those who oppose it, of the eventual passage of a Statehood act.

Then came the U.N. Decolonization resolution and much confusion resulted. But there is a change now with a belief that independence is more likely than ever in Puerto Rico's history or a 'Free Association' giving Puerto Rico more areas of sovereignty than it ever had.

Since the first political parties were formed under Spanish rule in the middle of the nineteenth century, and continuing throughout the years of American occupation until today, the question of the "status" of Puerto Rico has been the dominant theme of all. Parties have arisen and died; names have been changed, but fundamentally each one has been separated from the others according to its position in relation to that fundamental problem. For more than one hundred years, there has existed three differing ideological standpoints: assimilation, independence, or the continuation of ties to the existing power, Spain or the United States, with expanding degrees of self-government. This has been the basis for political division within Puerto Rico. It is heatedly debated as no other issue has been.

President Reagan and President Bush have both firmly said on many occasions that they will work for Puerto Rico to become the fifty-first state. However, some new factors have recently entered the picture. In 1980, after the most confused election in the island's history, Romero Barcelo became governor again by the tiny margin of 3,000 votes, while the P.D.P. won the majority of seats in the Senate. On the basis of the most recent elections, the Puerto Rican people as a whole, it would seem, do not want statehood.

Another new element in the situation is the conservative Right in the Reagan administration, which firmly rejects the notion of statehood for Puerto Rico. In consideration of this and other such problems, a proposal has been made to grant Puerto Rico independence, but with strings attached. One of these strings would be that the United States keep its base at Roosevelt Roads by paying a yearly rental. This plan would provide monetary help to Puerto Rico and would relieve the United States of any other financial obligation. It would be agreed that someone friendly to U.S. interests would be appointed as president. For a time, Puerto Ricans would have dual citizenship. Later they would have to choose between the two nationalities. Eventually, the flow of Puerto Rican immigrants into the States would stop. A decision by the United States for self-determination for Puerto Rico would have great propaganda value in the United Nations.

Which alternative, statehood or independence, will be chosen can only be guessed.

9
The People and Their Customs

SINCE the futures of Puerto Rico and the United States are related, Americans should know something of the island people. In many of the larger cities such as New York, Boston, and Chicago, there are sizeable enclaves of Puerto Ricans. For the most part, they live in poor conditions in ghettos, and the average American has little chance of knowing them. Too, they are conditioned by their environment and often act and appear differently from what they would in their native milieu. The changes wrought in those who have lived in the States for a length of time are recognized by their countrymen, so that they are called *Neoricans.* Most of them, however, do wish to return to their sunny native land if opportunity and work were open to them on the island. In this respect, they differ from other immigrant groups to the States. For most, Puerto Rico is home, where they have relatives and friends and where they are understood and where they can speak their own language.

There are over one million Puerto Ricans living in the States. For twenty years, between 1952 and 1972, half a million left the island for the States. There was an average migration of about twenty thousand people a year. Now that is changing and Puerto Ricans are coming home. They make what money they can, and then return. Sociologists find those in particular who were born on the island, desire to come back.

There is a story told of Puerto Ricans telephoning record stores in their locality, which have a record of a "coqui" making its night noises (the "coqui" is a tiny tree frog unique to Puerto Rico) and asking for it to be played over the telephone. This story reveals their deep nostalgia for their home. There are other reasons, too, for their wish to return—personal and economic ones. Discrimination against them, violence in the ghettos, and the cruel winters are some reasons why they are driven back to their island. Now the flow back is about twenty thousand Puerto Ricans a year, almost exactly duplicating the earlier flow of the previous two decades to the States.

An "urbanization" just outside San Juan, Levittown, has a mainly "returnee" population. So does the large industrial center of Bayamon. The Neoricans, used to the rush of the big cities of Chicago and New York, often find it difficult to adjust to the slower tempo of life on the island, and many of the young ones have to learn Spanish.

Some interesting comments on the people of Puerto Rico were made by Charles Emerson, brother of Ralph Waldo Emerson, when he had visited the island to escape the rigors of a Boston winter in 1833. He told many New England audiences that "They are a people

"Spanglish" by the oceanside with a chair and umbrella under which to keep cool, the middle-aged owner sells hamburgers and hot dogs and "Refrescos del Pais" (Puerto Rican drinks) (PHOTO BY MARTIN SAMOILOFF, JR.)

of beautiful manners. Their courtesy seems to be a constituent part of their language—we know, however, that the character of a language is only a reflection of the character of the people who speak it."

Some changes in language, of course, have occurred during the years, so that the Spanish spoken in Puerto Rico is not exactly the same as that spoken in Spain, its original source, or as in Colombia or in the Dominican Republic. These, however, are regional differences in language which occur even in one country, such as between the South and New England in the States. Also in recent years, some English words have appeared in the language and are generally accepted colloquialisms. Some people have designated the practice of using English words in a Spanish sentence as "Spanglish." It is particularly prevalent in the language of the Neoricans. But in almost all countries of the world today, Americanisms and Anglicisms have entered the language. For instance, in France, "le sandwich" and "le weekend" are perfectly permissible—except to purists.

The people of Puerto Rico are warmhearted and responsive. These are qualities that are becoming rare, especially in highly industrialized countries. The alienated person is becoming widespread. However, in Puerto Rico, warmth and liveliness are still to be found in a people whose roots are still in the land, whose bonds to their natural surroundings have not yet been completely broken.

For instance, in greeting each other, men will throw their arms about their friends' shoulders and hug them. It is not unusual for men to show their affection by kissing each other on the cheeks. Between business associates a handshake is the form; between friends an "abrazo." An American or English boy or young man, for instance, will almost never kiss his father. A son in Puerto Rico will kiss his father as well as his mother daily.

Women kiss and embrace each other almost as a matter of course, and little girls kiss older women, whether related to them or not.

There is a great use of the hands as a means of expression. Those speaking on television, giving a lecture or a speech, will use their hands to help express what they are saying. The hands are in constant use, and the number of ways they are used is as varied as those of a musical conductor. They will also shrug their shoulders, open wide their arms, and shake their heads as means of expression. With any sound of music their bodies respond almost automatically with a tap of the foot or a slight swaying of the body.

There is a genuine neighborliness, especially among the poor. In the slum areas of the big cities in the States, where the conditions breed distrust and suspicion, it is like a jungle, where man's hand is against another. But in Puerto Rico, neighbors take care of each

other. If one man is out of work, or if a family is in trouble in any way, friends and relatives help out. Despite the depressing picture that *La Vida,* Dr. Oscar Lewis's book, gives of the cultural poverty existing in the slums of San Juan, this custom of the poor helping the poor is still present.

A young American wrote in the Sunday edition of the *New York Times* of his experience in crossing the length of Puerto Rico, over the mountains, with just a knapsack on his back. There was hardly a time when he sat down to rest that someone did not venture forth from an isolated shack to offer him food. One old man insisted on going into his yard, twisting the neck of a chicken, and having his wife prepare it to share a meal with a stranger. On another occasion, he awoke one morning from his sleeping bag to find a shy little girl with a plate of rice and beans in her hands to offer him for his breakfast. Puerto Ricans are as generous as Columbus found their Taino ancestors. Invariably if a stranger shows good will, this type of responsiveness and generosity will be shown to him or her.

There is an everyday saying, "Mi casa es su casa." (My house is your house.") At Christmas time, there may not be any snow or traditional Christmas decorations, though these latter are now appearing, but hospitality is widespread. All houses are open to friends for food and drinks and music and gaiety.

The gaiety of Puerto Ricans is very real and spontaneous. They laugh and joke with each other easily.

Equally, they are quick to get into passionate rages. They get excited over arguments. Their "dignidad" is quickly offended. Over drinks in a bar, a knife may be pulled out quickly. A fight can ensue over a triviality. A psychiatrist and a lawyer discussing the question of violence in Puerto Rico today, agreed there is little mass violence. (People on strike usually carry their pickets around in smiling fashion). Both experts thought that much of the individual violence rose out of the present confusion about national identity.

Godparents have particular importance in Puerto Rico. Called "compradrazgo," roughly meaning comradeship or close friendship, it entails a duty on the part of the godparents to take care of his or her godchild should any unfortunate happening or the death of the parents occur. A godparent is supposed to have an almost kinship relationship with the child, give him or her presents on Saint's Days and birthdays, and Three Kings' Day, and have a sense of responsibility towards the child.

"Machismo" has always been a great feature with Puerto Rican men. This is the show of their manhood. They will fight each other with knives if they are angry enough. There have been reports of

A typical little Puerto Rican girl and boy today. Both show the racial blend of their forebears. Children have the security of extended family relationships. (PHOTO BY SAN JUAN STAR.)

killings over what may seem trivial affairs to outsiders. Very often it will be over a woman. Not to have more than one woman is almost a sign of lacking virility. Friday nights are called "Viernes Sociales," evenings when a man takes out his mistress. Saturdays are days spent with his wife and children. A man's children may be of two women. Sundays are spent with his mother and the larger family group.

If the woman keeps the children when a man leaves her, she is likely to return to her own mother, who will act as baby-sitter while the woman goes out to work. A common-law wife is not unusual and no child is considered illegitimate. There is also the extended family to which the child will belong if something happens to his parents. Though a Catholic country, the divorce rate is high.

In Puerto Rico, there are a great number of common-law marriages, that is, relationships where there has been no marriage ceremony. Sometimes this is because the man is running two households. The children of such unions are not in any way victimized as illegitimate. A child in such a situation is seldom sent to an orphanage. If the father does leave the mother, then she brings up the children herself, and it seems to be generally accepted that she can go back within her own family group again. In this way, whatever the

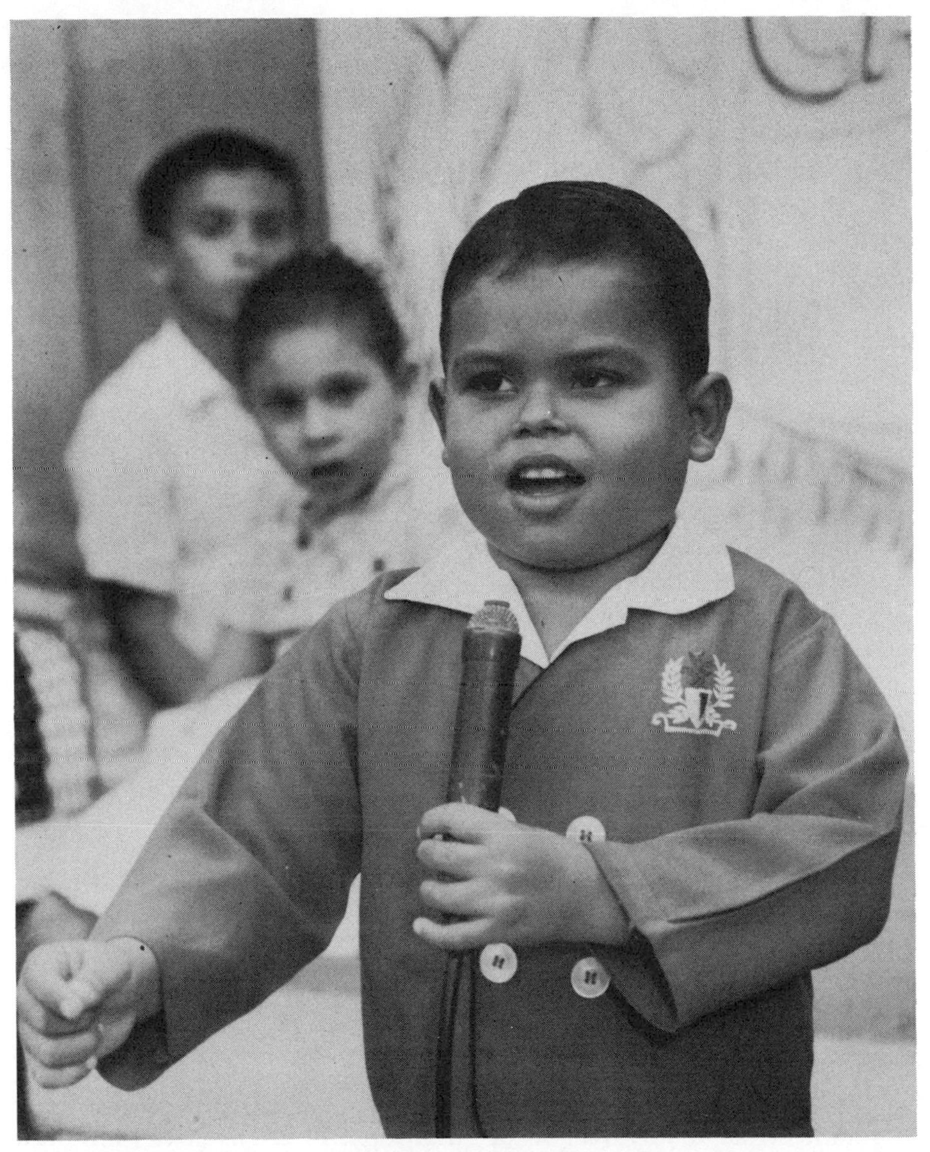

Puerto Ricans show great affection for their children. All dressed up and ready to become a radio announcer, this boy is a child of a typical Puerto Rican middle-class family. (PHOTO BY SAN JUAN STAR.)

mother's relationship with the father, the child always has substitute fathers in uncles. It always has grandmother, grandfather, and cousins, and so is not bereft of the security that family upbringing gives a child.

Every child in Puerto Rico is officially considered legitimate, and when he or she is born he or she is registered under both father's and mother's name. People in general use both father's and mother's name—the father's first and the mother's second. Luis Muñoz Marin's father's name was Muñoz. His mother's was Marin. Muñoz's father was Muñoz Rivera because his father was Muñoz and his mother Rivera. This is confusing at first because in the States a woman uses her maiden name as her first name and her husband's as a surname. But to address people correctly in Puerto Rico, the first name, such as Muñoz, is the proper one to use.

In Puerto Rico, then, the family, usually a big one, is important. It was the same with their Taino ancestors, whose tribes were mainly extended family relationships. To a child especially, this must give a sense of security. If anything should happen to the immediate parents, there is always the larger group to which he or she belongs. A child can always be sure of affection. The relatives will always arrange for one or another of them to look after the children in their own households with their own children. For adults, too, this sense of belonging must be of importance.

Here on the island a person knows that whatever happens, there are people close to him or her—family, relatives, friends—who will share in sorrows, pleasures, and successes. They will be there in times of sickness, happiness, succor him when he is sick, be happy when he is happy and sad when he is sad.

Perhaps because of the large family unit, the children all seem happy and have a great deal of security. Puerto Ricans show great affection for their children. They are pleasant, gay, young people. A group of children coming out of school at the end of a lesson period are all laughing and playing.

Certainly to see the children come out of school is to feel they are not oppressed in school. On a school bus a group of children, boys and girls, will chatter noisily. On a bus, a small girl or boy will give up his seat for an older person. Most of the children have this natural and pleasing politeness toward older people.

A black child in Puerto Rico grows up freely. He or she knows there is very little bar to any dreams or ambitions. There are blacks in high places in the Legislature, in the police department, in the schools, and in the Civil Service—in fact, at all levels of executive and managerial positions. A child hears the names of black governors and heads of state on the islands around him in the Caribbean such as: Eric Williams in Trinidad, Michael Manley in Jamaica, Baby Doc Duvalier in Haiti, Forbes Robertson in Guyana. In all society, even in one's own family, there may be every shade of skin from black to white, and this is reflected in the press, the magazines, and on television.

The blacks today represent about ten percent of the total population of two and a half million. After the slave ships stopped bringing

Near the modern Norte Centro *shopping center, a small boy rides the cart built for him by his father and pulled by the family dog. The boy has eleven brothers and sisters. Dog and boy look happy, like most Puerto Rican children. A black child in Puerto Rico grows up freely.* (PHOTO BY SAN JUAN STAR.)

in their human cargo from Africa in 1813, the influx of blacks more or less ceased.

Nevertheless, despite the mixing of the races over four centuries, there is now some veiled discrimination against blacks in Puerto Rico. A middle-class lady will take a parasol when she walks in the sun to prevent her skin from becoming a darker shade. In the job market, the large number of black Puerto Ricans, tend to be on the lowest rungs.

The great majority of immigrants during the last century and a half were mostly Spaniards or South Americans, and this has produced the present predominantly light olive or cream colored Spanish type creole or mestizo. Indeed, the majority would appear to be similar in coloring and physiognomy to those first inhabitants the conquistadors found in the early sixteenth century; a small statured handsome race of light brownish hue with straight black hair and dark eyes.

As well as Spaniards, Africans, pirates, and others from different nations, Puerto Rico has had a good quota of refugees. During the last century, refugees were mostly French families fleeing from Haiti and the successful revolution of Toussaint L'Ouverture, the Black Emperor. There were also Spanish royalists escaping revolutions in South America. Some Americans also came, notably French Catholics from Louisiana and Irish Catholics from Philadelphia who did not want to remain in a Protestant country. Forty years ago the refugees were mostly Spaniards escaping from Franco, and Germans and Austrians escaping from Hitler. The most recent refugees have been Cubans fleeing from Castro. And, of course, Americans have come in ever-increasing numbers during the last few decades.

The American colony, exclusive of army and navy personnel, now numbers about 50,000, although 1,000,000 Americans also come each year to the island as tourists.

Intermarriage between brown and white, brown and black, and white and black, has been common for the last 450 years. So there have been produced many mixtures of color. In marriages originally of blacks and whites, first-generation mulattoes are usually of intermediate color. In the second generation, there is greater variety, with some black, some "almost" white, some brown children. In Puerto Rico and other countries where there is intermarriage, each generation produces different gradations of color.

It is to be expected that mixed marriages, having been commonplace here for several centuries, would be still common today. The American and European men continue the tradition of Spaniards in marrying Creole and black women. In the past, however, white men, almost exclusively, married or lived with black and native women. Today, there is a new situation, with white women also marrying Puerto Rican and black men.

It is obvious that mixed marriages are widespread here and are as generally accepted now as they always were.

As far as their children are concerned, Theodosius Dobzhansky, the eminent biologist, wrote: "The variety of human genotypes, and hence of inclinations and abilities, is increased, not decreased by hybridization. I suppose the same is true on the cultural level also."

A Puerto Rican man is less likely to break up his home and go off with another woman if he has a family. He may have and often does have affairs, but he will tend to stay permanently anchored to his wife. However, despite being a Catholic country (actually, although eighty percent of the population are Catholic, only about twenty percent are practicing Catholics), a divorce is fairly easy to obtain in Puerto Rico. Among the poor, if a man takes a second wife, it will usually be without benefit of the Church, but in the middle classes there are many divorces and remarriages.

Women "libbers" are a minority. Most Puerto Rican women want to look pretty, feminine, and pleasing to their men.

In the past, a factor that had important implications for family life was the habit of siesta. In the middle of the day, all work closed down for at least two hours. The father went home and the midday meal was taken together by the parents and the children. Even now the father is certainly no stranger in the home or to his children, as so many men are in the States. It is common in the States for fathers to leave the house early in the morning and arrive back late at night. He is also absent because of frequent business trips. The Puerto Rican father's presence is felt and he is respected as head of the family.

Though some stores still close at noon it is usually only a work stoppage of one hour. Other firms, especially American ones, no longer have any shut-down period during the day, and the time-honored siesta for working and professional people is becoming a habit lost to the past. This is having its effects on the old patterns of family life. Still life for many is still leisurely.

Due to recent industrialization of the island, there have been other breakdowns in the family relationships. The light industry that has

The owner stands at the door of his grocery store (colmado) *to see what is passing in the one-way street* (transito). *Life is leisurely, there is always* manana *(tomorrow).* (PHOTO BY MARTIN SAMOILOFF, JR.)

A tiny homemade table holds a few coconuts for sale while the two men wait patiently sitting on a wooden crate by the dockside in Old San Juan. They have no office hours. (PHOTO BY MARTIN SAMOILOFF, JR.)

been established here, such as the manufacture of bras, uses women workers. This has an effect, of course, on the society as a whole, and on such questions as unions. But it is noticeable particularly in the relationship of the Puerto Rico woman to her husband. The fact that she has become a wage earner, and is sometimes bringing in a greater wage than the man, does tend to undermine his old role as head of the family.

Another factor which is changing Puerto Rican life is birth control and sterilization. It is no longer common for a woman to have sixteen or twenty children as was the case twenty years ago.

The question of abortion is a hotly debated issue, strongly disapproved by the Church even in cases of rape. As in the States, demonstrations against abortions have been held.

However, despite these cracks in the structure of society, the family still remains the important center for most Puerto Rican individuals. Men have a tremendous respect for their mothers—often more than for their wives—grandmothers—"abuelas"—are also important.

A vendor has his stand and chair under an umbrella in old San Juan. The blue stones of the roadway in the foreground were brought in as ballast by Spanish sailing ships. (PHOTO BY MARTIN SAMOILOFF, JR.)

Should the wife go out to work, her mother fills her place, rather than a baby-sitter or a stranger paid to take care of the children.

The Puerto Rican day begins early. People get to work at 8:30 A.M. and leave at 4:30 P.M. It means that even when both the parents work they still have a reasonable number of hours in the evening to spend with the children.

Puerto Ricans greatest pleasures are in 'fiestas,' but there are other enjoyments. Puerto Ricans like to gamble. There is a weekly government-run lottery. Also there is a new track on the outskirts of San Juan called El Commandante. Horse racing has always been a particular sport on the island. In the eighteenth century, part of the fiesta in honor of the patron saint of San Juan, St. John the Baptist, was horse racing through the narrow streets. One legend is that in 1753, one young man too late in making the turn at the end of one street overlooking the ocean, plunged to his death, some say, others that he was saved. A small chapel built by grateful parents according to those who say he was saved now blocks the way. Horseracing is no longer included in the festivities. The special horse of Puerto Rico is

A honeymooning couple share a horse in the hills of Puerto Rico. Paso finos, *the island horses have a distinctive dainty gait.* (PHOTO COURTESY OF PUERTO RICO TOURISM DEVELOPMENT.)

A Puerto Rican lobsterman mending his langusta *nets on a beach near Fajardo, Puerto Rico.* (PHOTO COURTESY PUERTO RICO TOURISMO DEVELOPMENT.)

As the sun sets, the fish begin to bite off the piers in San Juan harbor. Both casting tackle and hand-lines will get bites. Fishing is a sport as well as a means of livelihood. (PHOTO COURTESY PUERTO RICO TOURISMO DEVELOPMENT.)

the "paso fino," a small, delicate horse with a dainty, gait.

Puerto Ricans are both "béisbol" (baseball) and basketball ("baloncesta") fans. Each town has its own teams and rivalry is fierce. Many Puerto Ricans make the Big Leagues in the States. In other sports, there is Charles Pasarrel, the tennis champion, and "Chichi" Rodriguez, the golf champion. In memory of Roberto Clemente, a huge sports stadium has been built in San Juan. There are also a number of champions in the boxing and wrestling fields. In the Olympics, Puerto Ricans play as part of the United States teams and not separately.

Fishing is a sport as well as a means of livelihood for men and boys. A few miles off shore, there is deep sea fishing for marlin, swordfish, barracuda, sailfish and the rest of the big fish. Whales and porpoises are seen frequently in the ocean. There are sharks occasionally, but they seem to keep beyond the outer reefs that ring Puerto Rico. There is all kinds of boating, skiing, snorkeling, and surfing in the rough seas. The beaches for bathing (and all beaches are public by law) are mostly coves with a gentle surf.

The youth of the island engage very much in the same pastimes as their counterparts in the States. They like dancing and loud rock music. If they own cars, they enjoy racing around in them. About ten or fifteen years ago, there was no drug addiction on the island. Now it

This is part of the fishing laboratory in Mayaguez. Marlin, bonito, sailfish, swordfish, shark, and other big fish of the sea are caught in these waters. (PHOTO COURTESY OF U.S. DEPARTMENT OF AGRICULTURE.)

Fishing boats and pleasure motor boats at La Paguera, the "Phosphorescent Bay," one of the few such bays in the world. (PHOTO COURTESY OF U.S. DEPARTMENT OF AGRICULTURE.)

is rife as well as the high crime rate that accompanies it. Much of the drug trade is brought in from New York and Miami. The forty per cent unemployment rate among the young, also contributes to the crime rate. Today in San Juan and its suburbs, every house has "rejas," iron grillwork to keep out burglars. In the countryside, it is different, and doors do not have to be locked.

Among the women, there is great interest in dress. School children wear uniforms—the girls white blouses and white socks with a dark colored skirt; the boys, white shirts and dark pants. The uniform colors are different for different schools. Once beyond school age, the young dress in the brightest mixture of colors. They add to the brightness of the Puerto Rican scene. They love clothes and a great deal of money, when available, goes into buying clothes. In the upper brackets, there are many Puerto Rican fashion designers such as Fernando Pena and Designer Katin and exhibitions of their special designs.

For the working man, a large straw hat, old dark-colored pants and an open shirt are customary. For best occasions a "guayabera," a loose short-sleeved, open-necked, highly embroidered shirt is worn over long pants. Unlike tourists or American residents, however hot the weather, Puerto Rican men do not wear "shorts." When married, the women still wear bright dresses, but their clothes are more sedate than those of young girls. Pantsuits, especially among factory workers, are much favored despite the hot climate.

Most Puerto Rican women wear earrings. Nearly all baby girls have their ears pierced early. A fan used to be part of the social equipment of a woman, as well as a "mantilla" to wear to church. These are seldom seen today. The ex-mayoress of San Juan, Dona Felisa, a charismatic figure in her time, has a great collection of fans. She can expound on the manner in which the different ways they were fluttered could convey different signals to enamoured swains.

While American food is now eaten on the island, there are many typical Puerto Rican dishes. Also, in huts on the road near the airport and outside Luquillo beach and other public places, special Puerto Rican foods can be bought. Fruit that is brought in from the countryside can also be bought. However, since food is bought in the big supermarkets or in the "barrios," there are few open markets. There are however, small neighborhood enterprises where the local people can usually buy on credit. These are called "colmados."

Rice is a staple in Puerto Rican diet. Rice and beans are a traditional dish. Then there is *arroz con pollo,* rice with chicken, *arroz asapa,* a thick soup with rice and chicken or meat. Rice is used also in different ways with fish and sea food. *Pasteles* with various ingredients are mixed

Paradora Gripinas, high in the mountains, is a restored coffee plantation house. Its small kitchen prepares a menu of authentic Puerto Rican dishes. (PHOTO COURTESY OF PUERTO RICO TOURISM DEVELOPMENT.)

with meat, wrapped in plantain leaves and cooked. *Bacalaitos* are fried cod fish cakes. Roast pig is a national fare. Along the roadside are glassed in ovens where pigs are roasted on turnspits and sold to customers, who stop by to eat them. A pig roasted outdoors on a spit is essential for any party. In Bayamon in particular, but in other parts of the island too, roasted pig skin, "chicharrón" is sold from pushcarts. For dessert, there are *besitos de coco, pudin,* and *flan. Arroz con habichuelas* (rice with beans) is served almost daily. Instead of potatoes, fried plantains are served. This is the big green banana-

A vendor of newspapers and refreshments has a shack next to La Parada Colmado (the "Stop" grocery store). The Colmado is always open and gives credit in the neighborhood. (PHOTO BY MARTIN SAMOILOFF, JR.)

like fruit used as a vegetable. Mangoes, avocadoes, breadfruit, and sweet potatoes, uniquely served and cooked, are among items that are on Puerto Rican menus. Many dishes are highly spiced since red peppers are often added, as well as garlic and onions.

Seafood is a Puerto Rican favorite: shrimps, lobster, turtles, crabs—both sea crabs and land crabs. The land crabs live in the roots of the mangrove (a tropical maritime tree), and also burrow in the ground in houses close to the water. Small boys, as well as men, set traps for them, with a piece of coconut as enticement. A dozen of them strung on a string are hawked by the small boys along the roadside. They are ugly looking, but Puerto Ricans consider them a delicacy.

Puerto Ricans bake a special tasty bread. It is called "pan de aqua" and made in long thin loaves, similar to a French-style loaf. There is a special cheese, "queso de pais" made from goats' milk and eaten with guava jelly.

Ice cream is a favorite as it is everywhere, but ice cream in Puerto Rico is made from the fruits of the island: coconut, guanabana, guava, banana, mango, pineapple.

Ice cream vendors sell their wares from carts. They compete with the "piragua" man who sells from paper cones slivered ice over which he pours a fruit syrup from his array of bottles.

As with ice creams, there are special alcoholic drinks made from the island's fruits: banana daiquiris, mango daiquiris and piñacolada. Piñacolada is made of crushed ice, pineapple juice, and the cream and shavings of coconut and rum. Muy delicioso! Very delicious.

Libraries are rather poor in Puerto Rico towns, few in number and few in books. Except for the university libraries, in San Juan, there is only the endowed Carnegie Library and a Volunteer's Library mostly manned and equipped by American volunteers.

There are also few bookstores except in San Juan, where there are a number of good ones. Some carry books in both languages, by American, Puerto Rican, South American, Spanish, and other European writers.

There is a Sociedad de Autores Puertorriqueños (Society of Puerto Rican authors) which holds a number of literary events and promotes local authors. The supermarkets, drug stores, and such stores as Woolworth's stock popular "paperbacks"—mostly American books. They also carry newspapers, periodicals, and magazines. These again are both English and American publications, in both languages.

Among newspapers, there is the English language daily, The *San Juan Star,* and the Spanish language newspapers, El *Neuvo Dia,* El *Mundo,* El *Imparcial,* and El *Vocero,* and the "independentista," *Claridad.*

There are some excellent journals of high-quality content published, such as *Inter-American Revista,* and the *Caribbean Studies Review.* These carry articles in both Spanish and English by authorities on a range of scholarly subjects. There is also a literary journal in Spanish, *Sin Nombre.*

The radio stations naturally broadcast in Spanish, except for one English-language station. They all broadcast news, talks, and music. One station has a program of classical music that lasts for several hours.

Television networks provide such fare as soap operas, comedies, sports, news, "Cannon," "Kojak," and American movies dubbed in Spanish. There are some movies synchronized with radio so that by tuning in, it is possible to hear the text of the movie in English. There is one Public Broadcasting station that shows the "B.B.C. Masterpiece Theatre Series," an occasional National Geographic Society film, and the "Casal Festivals." Cable TV exists in San Juan.

Every town has its own Saint and its own Saint's Day. This entails a week long fiesta. The fiesta at Loiza Aldea is the most popular and the most colorful.

A Palm Sunday procession starts out from the steps of the church at San Mateo, Puerto Rico. (PHOTO COURTESY OF PUERTO RICO TOURISMO DEVELOPMENT.)

The fiesta in Loiza Aldea in honor of the apostle Santiago, when Spanish "caballeros" in plumed hats and frilled pants fight a mock battle against the Moors. (PHOTO COURTESY OF INSTITUTO DE CULTURA PUERTORRIQUEÑA.)

Two masked figures with bat-like wings amongst the costumed men and women at the fiesta in Loiaz Aldea. (PHOTO COURTESY OF INSTITUTO DE CULTURA PUERTORRIQUEÑA.)

Each of the traditional costumes of the Loiza Aldeans has a special significance. There are the finely dressed Spanish gentlemen, *los caballeros,* whose role is that of the Christian Crusaders. Then come the Moors, *los rejigantes* with frightening horned masks and wearing loose outfits with bat-like sleeves. Next, there are the old men, *los viejos,* and accompanying them men dressed as women, who act wildly

San Juan Bautista Day is the occasion for a Puerto Rican "Mardi Gras." Here one beautiful Puerto Rican butterfly stands on a float in a huge parade through San Juan. (PHOTO COURTESY OF PUERTO RICO TOURISM DEVELOPMENT.)

and are called the crazy ones, *los locos.* The fiesta takes place from July 23 to August 1, and is in honor of Santiago, the Spanish knight who helped drive the Moors from Spain. A popular legend tells of an old fisherman who found a statue of the saint on the beach. Though the local priest refused to bless the small image since Saint Patrick was the town's patron saint, Santiago soon became the central figure for the local fiesta. It has been suggested that most of the blacks arriving in this area were from the Yoruba tribe, who had a warrior god Shango, and that Shango and Santiago became intertwined in the minds of the slaves. In any case, it is the most festive and colorful of all the towns' celebrations, and one in which the drums beat most loudly.

Everyone on the island takes part in "San Juan Bautista" day.

Families crowd into whatever vehicle is available to take them to the beach. Decorative lights and platforms for musicians are erected. Many younger people put up tents intending to stay all night. Food and drinks are bought for late supper. Then at midnight everyone goes into the water fully dressed. The ritual is to walk in backwards into the water three times. This is to bring "suerte," luck, for the whole of the coming year.

Puerto Ricans celebrate American holidays, such as July 4 and Memorial Day. There are also special Puerto Rican holidays dedicated to the island's patriots. Most people enjoy them just as holidays, but they are also occasions for political demonstrations. Emancipation Day is celebrated on March 22, for the day in 1873 when slavery was abolished on the island. July 25 is Constitution Day, celebrating the day Puerto Ricans had their first constitution in 1952. The Church also has special days for the celebration of special ceremonies and Masses. Despite the fact that Puerto Rico is eighty-five percent Catholics, only about twenty percent regularly practice their religion. For most, the Church is there for weddings (though common law marriages abound), for christenings, confirmations, occasional confessions, and funerals. Funerals are always well-attended with a procession from the church to the cemetery. When cars cannot be afforded, the coffins are carried on men's shoulders through the streets.

Among Catholics, the Virgin Mary is held in greatest esteem. Any saint's day fiesta starts with a procession through the streets with the priest carrying a cross. Usually, there is also a banner with a painting of the Virgin or a statue of her carried by the people. One of the most famous shrines on the island is Our Lady of Montserrate, the dark virgin, dating from the early seventeenth century. "Ave Maria" (Hail Mary) and "Si Dios y la Virgen lo permiten." "If God and the Virgin permit it" are everyday expressions in Puerto Rico.

Many holidays in the States are different in many respects from those in Puerto Rico. One instance is the way that Christmas is celebrated. The Christmas holiday used to be held on Three Kings' Day (Epiphany, January 6) when the three kings, one of them black, riding on camels and guided by a star, sought the Christ Child. Puerto Rican children, on the night before, had always put straw under their beds for the camels. In return, they found presents there the next morning. But today, the shops and television programs are filled with toys and gifts from Santa Claus, who arrives on December 25. His reindeer gallop over snow which the children have never seen, and he comes down chimneys, which are nonexistent in their houses. Parents cannot afford to buy two sets of presents. The Archbishop of Puerto

Rico, recognizing the dilemma of the adults, has suggested the fusing of the two festivals into one to be held on Christmas Day.

Despite the Puerto Ricans changing world, which has led to a sense of loss of identity, there is still a strong core of feeling for "puertorrequeñismo," of being Puerto Rican. As with the Archbishops fusing the two holidays, the people mostly wish to feel that they are both Puerto Rican and American.

10
The Enchanted Island

PUERTO Rico, like most of the Caribbean Islands, is very beautiful. From the first discoverers, and throughout the centuries all who have seen Puerto Rico attest to its loveliness.

The young people wear T-shirts, and the older ones put stickers on their cars, proclaiming: *Puerto Rico me encanta* (Puerto Rico enchants me.) For despite the pollution that has accompanied industrialization, Puerto Rico remains what so often it has been called, "The Enchanted Island."

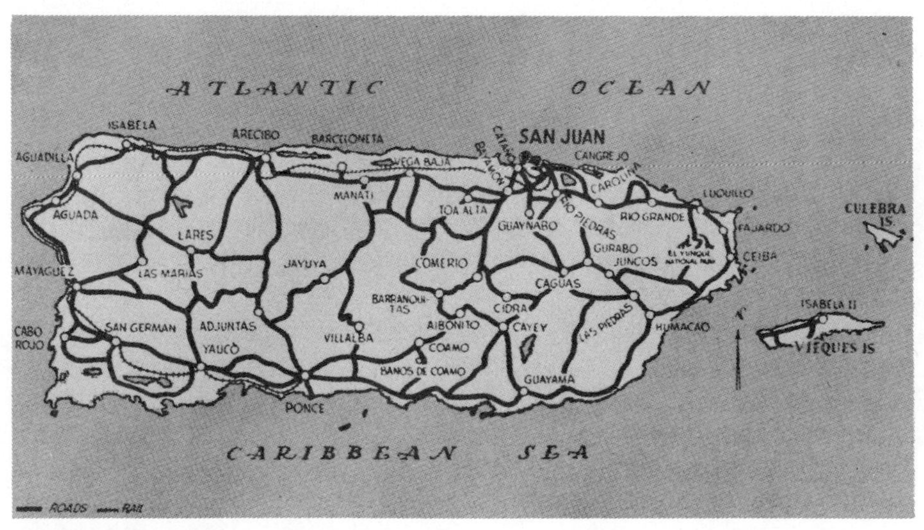

Map of Puerto Rico

One British landscape architect visiting here said he had never seen such variety of flora and fauna in such a small area. "This is a world treasure. We should keep it that way."

The country is really divided into four sections, each of them different, each offering its special beauty, and each having many different, and often unique, points of interest.

The south side tends to be hot and arid and the climate and vegetation are similar to that of Arizona. The west, with its good harbor with the Indian name of Mayaguez has the greatest rainfall, so the region there is very lush, vibrant with greens of every shade. Mona Island, off the west coast, is now practically uninhabited except for some weather stations. Wild boar and large iguanas are still to be found there. The Indians occupied it at first and then a mixed population. It became a favorite place for pirates and smugglers to put into port to obtain fresh fruit and vegetables. It has changed little in the intervening years except to become wild and uninhabited. For the future, it may be declared a National Park. Along the north coast, are the "Karst" hills which will be explained later. It is slightly to the

One of Puerto Rico's balnearios, *(developed public beaches) with picnic tables under the palm trees and Australian pines. By law, there are no private beaches on the island.* **(PHOTO COURTESY OF THE DEPARTMENT OF AGRICULTURE.)**

A little village nestled in the mountains of Puerto Rico. (PHOTO COURTESY OF PUERTO RICO INFORMATION SERVICE.)

Far off the beach are the reefs upon which waves break with a long white line of foam. Getting ready for the surf are two young men. (PHOTO COURTESY OF PUERTO RICO TOURISM DEVELOPMENT.)

east of these hills that San Juan, the capital, is situated. Off the coast of the rolling land of the east end lie the islands of Culebra and Vieques, which like Mona Island, are part of Puerto Rico. Until recently, Culebra was used as a target practice for the United States air force and navy, though some eight hundred people live there. Vieques is still used for U.S. air force and navy shelling practice.

All around the coast are palm-fringed beaches, fertile plains, and rolling hills. In the background everywhere are the mountains.

Travelling east along the old coastal road from San Juan to Loiza Aldea is to travel alongside palm-fringed sand coves and through quaint fishing villages. Here the coastal plain is green and soft, with cattle grazing in bamboo-shaded, flat meadows, adjacent to fields of feathery sugar cane. Alongside the ocean are crescents of sand ringed with coconut palms, beach plums, sea grapes, and tall Australian pines. The palms make bold strokes against the bright blue sky; the pines add contrast with their soft smidge of feathery green, and the beach plums spread their branches of round leaves at a lower height.

Way out are reefs upon which the waves break with a long white line of foam. The sea, a deep ultramarine, is streaked with emerald green. The scene outdoes picture postcards because it is real. The sun shines very brightly, almost every day, making the landscape sharp and clear.

A fifty-year survey shows that Puerto Rico has only five days a year totally without sunshine. There may be a heavy shower but the bright sunshine always follows. Even in the rainy season of May and November, there is seldom more than a day or two when it rains without cease. The temperature averages 75° F in the winter and 90° F in the summer. In some sea-level areas, summer can be very warm with considerable humidity. The mountain regions are always 10° F cooler than the coastal regions.

The coastal road from San Juan out to Loiza Aldea goes past the El San Juan and Americana hotels, then past the Isla Verde public beach to Boca de Congrejo, "the mouth of the crab." This is an opening from a densely tree-fringed mangrove lagoon into the ocean, where there is a large yacht club, and a bay where there are submarine gardens in which people snorkel.

After this, the good section of the road ends, and a dirt road begins to cut through a tremendous forest of tall coconut palms which edges the sea the rest of the way to the Loiza River. At first there are a few shacks where refreshments are sold, and here discarded beer cans and debris are in contrast with the natural beauty. Continuing, we come to an isolated community.

Early in 1500 African slaves were first brought to this point. It has remained a black settlement for all these years. In clearings, with the sun slanting through palm trees and tall Australian pines, are huts in groups of three or four, varying in appearance. Some are unkempt, but most are clean and tidy and show the prideful labor that has gone into their construction. All are obviously homemade with odd pieces of tin and wood, and roofs made of thatch of palm fronds.

All along the way, under forest trees that form a ceiling, magnificent as a Gothic cathedral, there are dazzlingly lovely views of the ocean in the blazing sun.

During the weekdays these coves are unoccupied because the men are at work, the older children at school, the women doing chores inside, and the babies, with the goats, pigs and chickens, are within the enclosures close to the huts. Here the beaches differ from those in the Isle Verde section. The sand is coarser and a stronger brown and gold, with shells here that are not found on other beaches. The coast must look as magnificent and unchanging as when Columbus and those first Spanish sailors landed in this New World.

The reefs are closer here, the waves breaking majestically, spraying high, glittering froth in the brilliant sunlight, then spilling and falling after reaching its peak.

At the end of the road, which covers some ten miles, is the Loiza River. There is a view of hazy, blue mountains, swathed in soft clouds. In the river estuary, where three hundred years ago the Spaniards extracted gold, men are fishing, standing in the waters and casting their big nets. On the other side is the small town of Loiza Aldea, one of the earliest settlements of the island. Cars are ferried across the river on a raft. A rope is stretched across the river, and two men drag the raft across by pulling on the rope, which also keeps them from swinging too far adrift in the current. Two planks are put up for the car to be driven carefully over and onto the floating raft. There is just enough room on the raft for one car and a few people, or two small cars. The men and women who live in the palm forest by the shore have to go to Loiza Aldea on this ferry in order to do their shopping, or to attend work, school, and worship.

The town is small and quiet with a sunny plaza. The usual benches and great trees surround it on four sides. The old Church of San Patricio stands on one side of the Plaza, facing a string of bars, shops and houses across the street. From here there are good roads and many small houses with pretty gardens.

Here along the road in tiny stores one can buy coconut masks with weirdly comic aspects such as horns, orange and black faces, and big tongues lolling from wide in twisted, grimacing mouths. Primitive paintings can also be had for a few dollars each.

The next point of interest is El Yunque, the mountain peak in the

In the shallows of the ocean the men are fishing, casting their big nets. (PHOTO COURTESY PUERTO RICO INFORMATION SERVICE.)

Luquillo mountain range, popularly known as the Rain Forest. It is the only tropical National Forest among the 150 United States National Forests. The mountain peak is about 3,500 feet above sea level. With the rainfall almost constant, the mountain is perpetually blanketed by clouds. This whole area of 29,000 acres is a National Park, developed during the depression years under the Puerto Rican Reconstruction Act. It has excellent motor roads up and down both sides of the mountain, as well as a series of well-laid paths for hikers. Near the top, there is a pool built among fernfestooned rocks, catching the water from one of the many waterfalls that glisten down blackened stone throughout the forest. The foliage is very dense with hundreds of different varieties of trees and bushes growing thickly together. Some of the 240 species of native trees, are survivers from an earlier geological age. There are fifty varieties of slender bamboos thirty feet high. There are also lacy fern trees, some as tall as two hundred feet, hardwoods, cedars, and mahogany. Here the laurel trees have the stature of great oaks. An undergrowth of tangled vines, heavy grasses, wild begonias, bromeliads and delicate tiny wild orchids grow in profusion.

The Puerto Rican parrot, one of the world's rarest birds. Columbus took about forty parrots with him to Spain after discovery of the Caribbean Islands. (PHOTO BY FRANK H. WADSWORTH.)

The quaint fishing village of Las Croabas, near Fajardo on Puerto Rico's northeast coast. Large turtles are among the catches. (PHOTO COURTESY OF PUERTO RICO INFORMATION SERVICE.)

A fishing boat cove on the island of Vieques, off the coast of Puerto Rico, is deserted in the afternoon. The U.S. Navy has taken over two-thirds of the island. (PHOTO COURTESY OF PUERTO RICO TOURISM DEVELOPMENT.)

A small native blue, green, and red parrot, one of the world's rarest birds, lives here. The forest itself is a bird sanctuary.

A pleasant restaurant with a wide verandah is situated near the top of the mountain. Here one can enjoy dinner and the wonderful view right down to the sea. From the very top of the mountain, it is possible to see the Atlantic Ocean on the one side and the Caribbean Sea on the other.

From El Yunque, the next place along the road is Luquillo Beach, one of the most beautiful beaches in the world. Its crescent of sand is also fringed by tall, coconut palms forever swaying in the trade winds. Fronting the beach is a well-landscaped park with lawns, flower beds, and many different varieties of crotons. The crotons are bushes which grow everywhere, with thick, glossy leaves of many shapes and colors.

From Luquillo, the road proceeds to Fajardo and Las Croabas. This is a small fishing town with many boats in its harbor. Here one can take ferries out to the islands that can be seen from Luquillo's shores. The islands, Vieques and Culebra, both belong to Puerto Rico. One can also ferry to the Virgin Islands of Saint Thomas and Saint Croix.

Vieques has an English-French background. The English filming of the movie *Lord of the Flies* took place here. Puerto Rico is now trying to develop its own film industry.

Today Vieques is a United States Marine Base, attached to Roosevelt Roads, the largest naval base in the Caribbean, where nuclear submarines dock.

Above, on the mountain behind Fajardo, is the El Conquistador Hotel with a spectacular view of the ocean and outlying islands on one side and low green mountains on the other.

There are three main highways on the island, numbered one, two, and three, as well as many new "autopistas" and expressways that connect with them. Highway I is the principal cross-island route over the mountains from San Juan to Ponce, but a recently built fast expressway is now more frequently used.

Highway 2 is the road westward through Arecibo and then on to Ponce. Highway 3 is the coastal road through Fajardo and on to Humacao and to Guayama, one of the prettiest towns, on the island and then to Ponce. All three highways start in San Juan. Off each of these three main highways are many secondary roads. So, though the island is only one hundred miles long and thirty-five miles wide, there are many places to be seen. Each one offers a different aspect of the island's scenery.

An aerial photograph of the Hotel Conquistador at the east end of the island with its spectacular ocean views.

Quiet serenity at the world-famous Dorado Beach Hotel in Dorado. (PHOTO COURTESY OF PUERTO RICO TOURISM DEVELOPMENT.)

Just outside San Juan, in Trujillo Alto are many "fincas" or farms. These fincas have been turned into country houses by middle-class families on good-sized areas of land. Here again is a different type of natural beauty. Below, stretches the silver streak of a river, which winds between high tree-festooned green hills. The scene is reminiscent of the country of the Rhineland, although without its boat traffic.

From Trujillo Alto a mountain route, through Gurabo goes down to Humacao and flat land; then, reaching Yabucoa, it goes up in the hills again to Vista Alegre (Joyful View). Going inland from any coastal point one always reaches the mountains.

To the west of San Juan, eighteen miles away, is Dorado (past a Puerto Rican Levittown). Dorado is situated along a curving road that has sweeps of beaches and the sunlit sea on one side and when in season, feathery grasses of sugar cane on the other. This part of the northern shore is where most of the sugar fields and "centrales," the sugar mills, are situated. At harvest time, the cut cane is carried piled high in trucks. Small boys pick up pieces that drop off to suck them like lollipops. In Dorado, a pretty, clean little town, is the Dorado Beach Hotel, which the Rockefellers used to own, and where Nelson Rockefeller has a house on the 1,760 acre hotel grounds. It was here, and in the adjoining Cerromar Hotel, used mainly for large conventions from the States, that Gerald Ford, when president, held a

A silo among the Karst hills on the northern plains of the island. (PHOTO COURTESY OF U.S. DEPARTMENT OF AGRICULTURE.)

summit conference, and where all the heads of state from Europe were housed.

Along the coast beyond Dorado, among many beaches, is Mar Chicquita, a particularly delightful fishing village. Its cove is almost completely ringed by a barrier of rocks which contains the ocean like a large blue pool, while the surf, thundering behind, hurls spray high into the air. Behind is the Karst country with its odd-shaped limestone hills, and conical holes, some over four hundred feet wide and 160 feet deep. The name *Karst* comes from Yugoslavia, where there are many of these conical holes (called "sinkholes") and small haystack hills. These curiously shaped holes and hills continue for quite a way along the North Shore going west. They are an interesting geological phenomenon caused by a solution of the soil through rainfall into conical "sinkholes" and then by deposits of the limestone forming hills. Below them near the ocean is the region where pineapples are grown. In the pineapple fields, the fruit is cut by hand, and the field hands carry big woven baskets of the fruit on their heads during a harvest time.

Here is a charming scene of ducks on a pond that could be a setting in a temperate climate, if it were not for the banana trees in the background. (PHOTO COURTESY OF AGRICULTURAL SERVICE, UNIVERSITY OF PUERTO RICO.)

Turning inland again from the coast, one begins the climb to the lower ridges of hills, green and gently sloping, offering scenes that could almost be duplicated anywhere in New England, and forming pastoral pictures similar to many places in temperate climates. Black and white cattle graze contentedly on the grasses and small houses nestle in the placid scene.

In these valleys and mountains of Aibonita was once found silver. (PHOTO COURTESY OF U.S. DEPARTMENT OF AGRICULTURE.)

Only here and there on the hillside, a few royal palms or some African "tulip" trees, tall as oaks and bright with flowers that do look exactly like red tulips, remind a stranger of the fact that he is in the tropics.

Climbing higher and higher into the magnificence of the Central Mountains, the "Cordillera Central," is the village of El Barranquitas. This is the birthplace and burial place of the famous political leader, Muñoz Rivera, father of the famous son, Muñoz Marin. Muñoz Rivera's house is now a museum open to the public. The little houses clustering on both sides of the mountain gap look, from a distance, like a group of colored boxes set down in a child's game. Higher still beyond the village, the old Hotel Barranquitas, with its charming setting of attractive landscaped grounds and a balcony with lovely vistas, is now a training school for hotel workers.

Still higher is an old inn, La Union de Todas, an unpretentious wooden structure where local farmers and country people take their families for midday dinner on Sundays for a truly Puerto Rican meal, eaten on bare, scrubbed wooden tables. When ex-President Betancourt was in exile from Venezuela for a number of years, he had many meetings with political sympathizers here in this inn. It is an isolated spot, with only an occasional shack or cottage to be seen on the opposite hills. One can watch a young child running down a steep incline with arms outstretched, taking obvious pleasure in her speed, or study an old peasant, "a campesino"—a "jibaro"—trudging sturdily and slowly up another narrow path to the hut that is his home.

Around bends in the road, through this central mountain range, new views open up, each one individually beautiful. Yet hovels clinging to the sides of the mountain are reminders that sixty percent of the population lives below the poverty line. The mountains, running the length of the island, east to west, form a backbone, and make up the second and perhaps most spectacular section of the island. Lakes lie in hollows between the peaks.

The three largest peaks are in the Toro Negro Commonwealth Forest, within a few miles of each other, lying north to south between Manatí and Ponce. There is Punta Peak (4,398 feet), the highest peak in Puerto Rico; Cerro Maravilla (Marvelous Peak), with an elevation of 3,800 feet; and Dona Juana Peak, which has an observation tower and a foot trail through a virgin palm forest.

A quiet lake—Lago Cidra—one of the many different aspects of the island's scenery. (PHOTO COURTESY OF U.S. DEPARTMENT OF AGRICULTURE.)

Dominoes is a game taken seriously in Puerto Rico, both by young and the old. Here in a quiet plaza, four men get shade and the fast pace of a game, always marked by quick clicks of the tiles. (PHOTO COURTESY OF PUERTO RICO TOURISM DEVELOPMENT.)

In small remote villages here as elsewhere, in plains or mountains old men sit outside tiny bars, little bigger than huts, and with a table between them, play the national game of dominoes. The game is played as seriously and takes as long as a game of chess. It is a pleasant way for old men to spend the day, a place too for friendly greetings and talk with friends who stop at the bar for a drink.

In the hill country, there are tractors used for cultivation as well as peasants pushing oxen up the steep slopes trying to force a living from the soil. On the roads, too, a jibaro may pass in his oxen-driven wooden cart. On many lower slopes cows and steers graze. There is a white cross-breed steer with a hump sired originally from a Brahmin bull.

Everywhere are little towns where the charm of the old Spanish architecture is still in evidence. Little gardens are alive with color, and the plazas are sleeping and deserted in hot afternoon sunshine.

In the little plots beside the huts and *cementos* there are no vegetable gardens, such as might be seen in the States. Here, perhaps as an expression of the native spirit, everyone grows flowers. The brightest flowers and shrubs grow in every garden, and even a spiky cactus is decorated with egg shells. The only utilitarian plant is a banana palm. Chickens, goats, and pigs roam in the yards, but there are few tomato or bean plants. This sort of husbandry is now mostly ignored by Puerto Rican jibaros because the supermarkets do not want to be bothered with small amounts of produce.

Arecibo Ionospheric Observatory in Arecibo. It is the largest in the world, built among the unique 'Karst' hills. It is under the supervision of Cornell University and astronomers from all over the world come to visit it. (PHOTO COURTESY OF PUERTO RICO INFORMATION SERVICE.)

Back along the coast, on the way to Arecibo are the centuries-old Indian caves with their pictographs and petroglyphs still to be seen. North of Arecibo near Utuado is the old Indian Ceremonial Park. This is the area where most archeological research is continued. Also near Arecibo is the largest radar-radio telescope in the world. The Ionosphere is operated jointly by Cornell University and the National Science Foundation. The reflector is placed in one of the natural Karst sinkholes and occupies over twenty acres with the aluminum bowl being 1,300 feet wide and three hundred feet deep. A platform running around the great reflector is suspended by cables from tall towers. Much scientific work in the field of astronomy is conducted in its research station. The tracking of Mars has been of particular interest. At nighttime here, the dark sky is studded with thousands of bright stars.

Nearby is that part of the island where coffee is grown. Coffee beans grow on shrubs that mature in three to five years. The red berries are handpicked and pulped to remove the two coffee beans inside each berry. These beans are then dried and sorted and packed in sacks.

In this area some underground caves have been discovered. Not all have yet been explored, but they are thought to be numerous and, surprisingly for this little island, are among the largest and most interesting in the world. Various national societies have sponsored expeditions to these caves and have published articles, including photographs, about them. The caves have been formed by a river flowing underground which comes up some miles later.

Among the great mountain peaks of the Cordillero Central, there is a big hydroelectric plant beside Lago Dos Bocas (the Lake of Two Mouths). Here and elsewhere, the government has used the water of many rivers to form man-made lakes to provide the electricity needed for homes, industry, and irrigation.

Traveling north and west along the coast, the hills come down close to the sea. There is greater rainfall here than in the San Juan area, so the vegetation is, if anything, greener and more lush, with flowers growing in ever greater profusion.

The shore here contrasts sharply with the soft, sandy, palm-ringed coves of the northeast. The coast is rocky and white-cliffed. In the countryside immediately inland, there are more than a hundred individual violet trees. In the ocean off the Balneario Guajataca (Guajataca Public Bathing Beach) may be seen porpoises or even occasional black whales.

The farthest point of the northwest corner at Aquadilla used to be Ramey Air Force Base. A fine school there was built for the American

In the hills near Jayuya is hacienda Gripinas, the former manager's residence for his coffee plantation. It is now restored and functions as one of many of the island's paradores *(small inns).* (PHOTO COURTESY OF PUERTO RICO TOURISM DEVELOPMENT.)

personnel and is still continued. The housing has been turned into tourists' villas and the hospital is also still in use.

The road turns left here entering into the western coastal plain: similar to the eastern plain, but with more rainfall. Mayaguez is the principal town. It used to be the embroidery center of the island now it is a center for the canning of tuna fish, the great fish being caught off its shore.

The highway is lined with royal palms, as is the entrance to the University of Puerto Rico's regional campus. The University is mainly devoted to engineering and the sciences. A U. S. Agricultural

Individual two- and three-bedroom villas are one of the many attractions of the Punta Borinquen resort area, a newly developed site on the west side of Puerto Rico formerly housing U.S. Air Force personnel. (PHOTO COURTESY OF PUERTO RICO TOURISM DEVELOPMENT.)

The small village of La Parguera sits sleepily in the afternoon sun, but at night this small fishing town on the south west coast comes alive. It is the site of the famous Phosphorescent Bay, and in the dark, a boat's wake gleams with watery fire. (PHOTO COURTESY OF PUERTO RICO TOURISM DEVELOPMENT.)

Experimental Station here has many exotic tropical trees and plants.

To the south is the town of Cabo Rojo, small and sleepy, with a yellow, turreted church. This was the birthplace of the Robin Hood pirate, Roberto Cofresi.

Along the road grows a gigantic "ceiba tree", one of the largest of tropical trees. It was of the great ceiba that the Indians made their large canoes and their drums.

The narrow lanes here are flanked by archways of trees, including the famous "flamboyan tree," which in July and August is covered with brilliant orange blossoms.

Boquerón on the southwest coast is a special public beach where cabins may be rented for days at a time. The area is well known for its oysters and other types of seafood as well as the many species of heron living in its mangroves. Below, is the Cabo Rojo Lighthouse. "Cabo Rojo" means red cape. Behind lies the Sierra Betmeja, low hills probably 130 million years old, and tinted red because of the iron oxide in the soil. Close by are salt flats, which appear like glistening snow mounds.

Along the southern shore lies the fishing village of La Parquera, with its phosphorescent bay, one of the few in the world. On a moonless night, a boat on the water will leave a golden wake. A hand dipped into the water will be withdrawn dripping with golden liquid. The luminescence is caused when a tiny species of marine life living in the water is disturbed. It is a most unusual phenomenon.

On a small island in the bay is an experimental station for research. Rhesus monkeys brought over from India, are allowed to live their lives freely among the trees, disturbed only by the occasional visit of the group of scientist who check up on their habits. Here the well-known Dr. C. R. Carpenter conducted his famous studies on primate societies.

This is part of the fourth distinct geographical section of the island, where nature assumes a still further change. Here in the south it is hot and dry, and there are often droughts. The pictorial scenes are quite different from those in the other sections. Here one is reminded of Arizona, or the Sierras of the southwestern states. Here grow the same cacti, including the prickly pear, and the same yuccas and mesquite trees, with yellow flowers and edible fruit. Greenness has been bleached out of the flat fields and the slopes; all is corn-yellow and seared. There are no forests here, only scrub, and the mountains are bare with an orange tint caught from the sun in the daytime, turning heliotrope in the twilight. It is lovely, but in a different way from the lush diverse greens of the other three areas.

Ponce, on the south shore, is the second largest town and second

A roof balcony in Old San Juan has its roofline softened by bougainvillea, Boston fern, and a variety of native hanging plants. (PHOTO COURTESY OF PUERTO RICO TOURISM DEVELOPMENT.)

largest port of the island. It has the distinction of having two charming Spanish-type plazas and, standing between them, the Cathedral of Our Lady of Guadaloupe, the first Church of England, in Puerto Rico and the Catholic University.

An interesting art museum, designed by Edward Durell Stone, has been donated by millionaire, ex-Governor, Luis Ferré, whose home is in Ponce. It houses his private collection of European and Puerto Rican paintings. On the coast nearby, the big oil refineries are located.

The Maguy *plant has thick, spiky leaves and grows to several feet in height.* (PHOTO COURTESY OF U.S. DEPARTMENT OF AGRICULTURE.)

In San German, inland on the southwest of the island, is a seventeenth century church which is perhaps one of the oldest in the hemisphere. It has been made into a museum for religious art. Known as Porta Coeli, it was built about 1600, and is one of the very earliest chapels either here or anywhere else in the Americas.

The main, and very pretty, campus of the Inter-American University, built on a hill, is here too.

Between San German and Mayaguez is the town of Hormigueros. A hundred steps lead up to the Sanctuary of Our Lady of Montserrat, and tales of miraculous happenings are told as part of its legend. Our Lady is a dark-complexioned Virgin.

Proceeding north again towards San Juan the roads wind continu-

One of Puerto Rico's many tropical plants has a waxy lily-like flower: a species of Maco. (PHOTO COURTESY OF U.S. DEPARTMENT OF AGRICULTURE.)

ously, first up, then down, then up again. At the high point, up about 4,000 feet, there are breathtaking views, one after another.

These mountain passes are especially lovely in spring and summer with flowers and blossoming trees everywhere, magnificent views in all directions, and cotton clouds moving across a vast blue sky to pattern the valleys below with sunlight and shadow.

There are flowers everywhere, among them red hibiscus (amapola) which is grown as a common hedge. The more exotic varieties are huge as a bread plate, with delicate coloring ranging from a pale gold to deep apricot pink. Then there are *oleanders,* of palest pink, white, cerise, and lavender. There are *canarios,* a yellow trumpet-like flower growing like a vine over fences or against the walls of the cottages and

A pleasing star-like plant given the poetic name of Song of India. (PHOTO COURTESY OF U.S. DEPARTMENT OF AGRICULTURE.)

houses. There are *Cruz de Malta,* the deep red or salmon pink so-called jungle geraniums. The *poinsettias* are large, many-blossomed bushes. *Bougainvillea* is many-hued and delicate as a sweetpea. Then there are the fragrant white *jasmine, birds of paradise, lobster claws, shrimp* plants, *ginger* and *arum* lilies. There are many other flowers with lovely names, such as "Golden Chalice," "Love's Chain," "Queen's Wreath," "Sky Flower," and "Angel's Trumpet."

Some of the prettiest gardens belong to owners of shacks. Whether rich or poor, if you have a love for flowers, you can enjoy them in profusion in Puerto Rico. Many of the trees are flowering too; the violet blue *jacaranda,* cassia (like apple blossoms), pink and white *acacias* (similar to cherry blossoms), and "Queen of the Flowers," which looks like a lilac tree.

Bromeliads grow on tree trunks and several times a year produce a bright red corn-shaped flower. (PHOTO COURTESY OF U.S. DEPARTMENT OF AGRICULTURE.)

Then there is the *bucaré* whose leaves fall off, so that only bright yellow flowers are on the branches; a "*chocoate*" tree which has strong pink blossoms; and the *aguabana* whose fruit, when mashed and chilled and mixed with milk, makes a most delectable milk drink. Then there are the groves of orange trees, grapefruit trees, and lemon and lime trees. All these have blossoms in season.

The coffee plants have an orchid-like flower. Its fruit is a crimson "cherry." The papaya tree is often about fifteen feet high with a few branches of sculptured leaves spreading almost horizontally near the top and, on the narrow trunk about halfway down, are football-size melon-like fruits. Luxuriant mango trees, heavy and full, rather like huge old oaks, hide green fruit amongst the foliage. The breadfruit

The beach at Icacos Island off Puerto Rico's northeast coast. It is an especially good spot for snorkelling and scuba diving, since the water is crystal clear. (PHOTO COURTESY OF PUERTO RICO INFORMATION SERVICE.)

trees, have beautifully shaped leaves, very large, dark, and shining like many-fingered hands. In the swampy land in the coastal areas, also, are the mangrove trees, stretching down their writhing roots deep into the water.

Compared to the abundance of flowers, tropical birds are not too plentiful. There are the water birds, the pelicans, the terns, the seagulls, and the herons. In the towns are doves and pigeons. In the plains, the tiny hummingbird with its irridescent feathers flies from flower to flower. There is the small "reineta," a yellow breasted bird who will fly into a house to steal sugar. A red-tailed hawk and turkey vultures are to be seen on occasions. The most popular bird is the island's "piterre". Near Mayaguez are two bird sanctuaries where there are over two hundred species of tropical birds.

There are no poisonous snakes on the island. There are mongoose, brought in to keep down the rats; a special variety being the coco-rat. Many lizards of all sizes and colors abound. Some quite big but there are no iguanas except on Mona Island. There are land crabs that burrow into the earth under houses near the water, and crabs that attach themselves to the mangrove trees. There are few spiders, but cockroaches, unless they are checked, infest houses and can grow as large as mice. In many residential areas, an exterminating service is used to keep homes free of them. There are mosquitoes, but spraying keeps them from being a nuisance, and screened windows and doors keep them from entering the houses.

There are many types of toads and frogs. The most famous, and unique to the island, is the little tree frog, as small as a fingernail. The call of numbers of them at night "coqui, coqui," provides an orchestra of sound almost like birds' songs.

The physical pleasures of the island are then obviously apparent—the warm waves and beaches, the softness of the air, the ever-present sunshine, the particular splendor of the clouds, the glowing sunsets, the benign skies of every day, the lush foliage, the flowers, the fruits, and the special atmosphere. Professor Robert D. Crossweller describes this in his book, "The Caribbean Community" by writing:

> "Even the products and the flora of the lands—coconut palms by the sea, sugar cane moving under warm winds, the scarlet berries and white flowers of the coffee trees approaching harvest, banana plantations astonishing in their sensuality—transcend the market place and find higher reality in a mythology of the tropics.
>
> "There is more to these assumptions of identity than mere imagination. There is indeed in the Caribbean the climate and mood and style of tropicality. There is the wide oceanic milieu of bright water and beach. There is the trade wind that blows over all things with unwavering constancy. There are the stabbing, crushing rains—there is a pace and tone of life, a curious blending of languor and passion, of excitement and unconcern that announces the tropics.
>
> "These felt sensations, crowding all about in the island Caribbean—are so evident that no one would mistake the Caribbean reality."

This reality is part of Puerto Rico's portrait too.

Bibliography

Aitkin, Thomas, Jr. *Poet in the Fortress, The Story of Lúis Muñoz Marin.* New York: The New American Library, 1964.

Arciniegas, German. *Latin America, A Cultural History.* New York: Alfred Knopf, 1969.

Blanco, Enrique T. *Los Tres Ataques Britanicos,* San Juan; Puerto Rico: Centero Fernandez y Co., 1947.

Blanco, Tomas. *Prontuario Historico de Puerto Rico.* Biblioteca de Autores Puertorriqueños. San Juan, 1949.

Chase, Stuart. *Operation Bootstrap; A Report on Progess,* 1951 Washington: Planning Pamphlets, National Planning Association, D.C. 1951.

Colorado, Antonio J. *The First Book of Puerto Rico.* N.Y.: Franklin Watts Inc., 1978.

Crassweller, Robert D. *The Caribbean Community,* New York: Frederick Praeger, 1972.

Cripps, L.L. Puerto Rico; *The Case for Independence,* Cambridge, Mass: Alfred Schenkman Co. 1974.

Cripps, L. L. *The Spanish Caribbean.* Boston, Massachusetts: G. K. Hall Co. 1979.

Cruxent, José M. and Rouse, Irving. *The Entry of Man Into The West Indies,* New Haven, Connecticut: Yale University Press, 1960.

Dahlberg, Edward. *The Gold of Ophir.* New York: E. P. Dutton & Co. 1972.

de las Casas, Bartolomé. *The Spanish Colonie.* London: Readex Micro-print from William Brome edition, 1583.

de Diego, José, *Neuvas Campañas y El Plebiscita: Obras Completas.* Rio Piedras, Puerto Rico: University of Puerto Rico.

Diaz Soler, Luis M. *Historia de la Esclavitud Negra en Puerto Rico.* Rio Piedras, Puerto Rico: Editorial Universitaria, 1896.

Diffie, Bailey W. and Justine. *Porto Rico: A Broken Pledge.* New York: The Vanguard Press, 1931.

Gorenstein, Shirley; Forbes, Pebard R; Tolstoy, Paul; Lansing Edward. *Pre-Historic America.* New York: St. Martins Press, 1974.

Gruber, Ruth. *Puerto Rico: Island of Promise.* New York: Hill and Wang, 1960.

Hanson, Earl Park. *Puerto Rico: Ally for Progress,* New York: Van Nostrand, 1962.

History of the Indians of Puerto Rico: San Juan, Puerto Rico: *Coleccion de Estudios Puertorriqueños,* 1970.

James C. L. R. *The Atlantic Slave Trade and Slavery.* New York: Penquin Books, 1970.

Jane C. (trans) *The Journal of Christopher Columbus.* New York: Potter and Co., 1960.

Konig, Hans. *Columbus: His Enterprise,* New York: Monthly Review Press, 1973.

Krickeberg, Walter, Triborn, Herman, Muller, Werner, Zerries, Otto. *Pre-Columbian American Religions.* London: Weidenfeld and Nicholson, 1965.

Lewis, Gordon K. *Puerto Rico: Freedom and Power in the Caribbean,* New York: Monthly Review Press, 1963.

Lewis, Gordon K. *Notes on the Puerto Rico Revolution.* New York: Monthly Review Press, 1974.

Lewis, Oscar. *La Vida: A Puerto Rican Family in the Culture of Poverty.* San Juan and New York: Random House, 1965.

Loven S. *Origins of Tainans Culture, West Indies.* Göteborg, Sweden, 1935.

Maldonado-Denis, Manuel. *Puerto Rico: A Socio-Historico Interpretation.* New York: Random House, 1972.

Mauncy, Albert and Torres Reyes, Ricardo. *The Forts of Old San Juan.* Riverside, Connecticut: The Chatham Press, 1973.

Martyr, D'Anghera, Peter. De Orbe Novo. The Gold of Ophir. New York: E. P. Dutton & Co. 1972.

Mathews, Thomas. *Puerto Rico: Politics and the New Deal.* Gainsville: University of Florida Press, 1960.

Mintz, Sidney. *The Culture and History of a Puerto Rican Plantation 1876-1969.* Hispanic American Review, 1953.

Mintz, Sidney. *Worker in the Cane.* New Haven: Yale University Press, 1964.

Miranda, Quintero Carmen. *On the Development of the People of Puerto Rico.* New York: Libro Libre, 1976.

Muñoz, Marin. *Breakthrough from Nationalism.* Harvard University: Harvard Godkin lectures, 1959.

Morales, Carrion Arturo. *Puerto Rico and the Non-Hispanic Caribbean.* Rio Piedras, Puerto Rico: University of Puerto Rico Press, 1952.

Morison, Samuel Eliot. *The European Discovery of America: The Southern Voyages, 1492-1616.* Oxford University Press, New York, 1974.

Negron, Aida de Montilla. *Americanization in Puerto Rico and the Public School System,* 1900-1930. Rio Piedras: Editorial Edil, 1971.

Safa, Helen Iaken. The Urban Poor of Puerto Rico. *A Study in Development and Inequality.* New York: Holt, Rinehart and Winston, 1974.

Silen, Juan Angel. *We, the Puerto Rican People.* New York: Monthly Review Press, 1971.

Stewart, Julian et al. *The People of Puerto Rico: A Study in Social Antropology.* Urbana, Illinois: University of Illinois, 1966.

Stuart, L. *Status of Puerto Rico.* United States and Puerto Rico Commission. Washington, D. C: U. S. Government Printing Office, 1966.

Thomas, Piri. *Down These Mean Streets.* New York: Alfred Knopf, 1967.

Tugwell, Rexford. Puerto Rico. *The Stricken Land.* Westport, Conn: Greenwood Press, 1968.

Wagenheim, Kal. *Puerto Rico: A Profile.* New York: Frederic Praeger & Co., 1971.

Wakefield, Dan. *Island in the City, Puerto Ricans in New York.* New York: Corwin Books, 1960.

Index